TOM MACKROLA

Practical Investor's Guide to Real Estate Investing

HOUSE MONEY PRESS

First published by House Money Press™, a division of ProfitSeas Publishing 2026

First edition

ISBN: 979-8-9994323-2-2

Contents

Introduction

The Practical Investor's Guide to Real Estate Investing

INTRODUCTION: Why This Book Exists

Most real estate investing books fall into two categories: they promise you'll get rich with no money down, or they're so technical you need a finance degree to follow along. This book does neither.

This is for people who want to build wealth through real estate without the hype, without the ideology, and without pretending it's easier than it is. You might be working a full-time job thinking about your first property. You might own two or three already and want to know what's next. Either way, you're looking for clarity, not cheerleading.

You're not here for motivational speeches about how real estate changed someone's life. You're here for practical information you can use. You want to know how deals actually work, what mistakes to avoid, and how to build a portfolio that generates income and grows wealth over time.

This book is written for investors who have jobs, families, and limited time. You're not trying to become a full-time real estate mogul. You're trying to build financial security through smart investments that don't consume your life.

The flow of this book is deliberate. We start with how investors actually think about money, risk, and return. Then we move into finding and analyzing deals. After that, we cover financing and property selection. Only then do we talk about operations and management, because you need to understand what you're signing up for before you scale. Finally, we address growth, exits, and how to work with the industry instead of around it.

Each chapter builds on the previous one. By the end, you'll have a complete framework for analyzing deals, avoiding mistakes, and building a portfolio that fits your goals.

Real estate rewards people who think clearly, move carefully, and stay flexible. This book will help you do all three.

1

Chapter 1: How Investors Actually Make Money

There's a quiet war in real estate investing circles: cash flow versus appreciation. Some investors swear by monthly income. Others chase equity growth. Both camps act like theirs is the only way that works.

They're both wrong.

Cash flow and appreciation aren't competing strategies. They're two sides of the same investment, and good investors pay attention to both. The difference is emphasis and timing.

Cash Flow Comes First

When you're starting out, cash flow matters most. It covers your mortgage, taxes, insurance, repairs, and vacancies. Positive cash flow means the property pays for itself and maybe puts a little extra in your pocket each month.

Appreciation is great, but you can't spend it until you sell or refinance. Cash flow is real. It shows up every month, and it funds the next deal.

Here's the thing: if you invest in markets and properties that generate solid cash flow, appreciation usually isn't far behind. Not always, and not immediately, but historically, cash-flowing properties in decent markets tend to gain value over time. You're not betting on appreciation. You're building a foundation that allows appreciation to work in your favor when it happens.

Cash flow gives you time. If you buy a property that generates $400 a month in cash flow and the market drops 20%, you don't have to sell. You can hold through the downturn because the property is still paying for itself. Eventually, the market recovers and you benefit from appreciation you didn't count on initially.

If you buy a property with no cash flow, hoping it will appreciate, and the market drops, you're in trouble. You're bleeding money every month. You can't hold indefinitely. Eventually, you're forced to sell at the worst possible time.

This is why cash flow comes first. It's defensive. It protects you when things go wrong.

Think of cash flow as your insurance policy against market downturns, bad luck, and unexpected expenses. It's what lets you sleep at night when property values dip or when you have a string of maintenance issues. Without cash flow, you're speculating. With it, you're investing.

Most failed real estate investors failed because they ignored cash flow. They bought properties that looked good on paper, assuming appreciation would bail them out. When the market softened, they couldn't cover the mortgage. They sold at a loss or lost properties to foreclosure. All because they prioritized potential appreciation over actual cash flow.

The investors who survived and thrived were the ones whose properties paid for themselves every month. When the market crashed in 2008, cash-flowing properties kept generating income. Owners could hold through the downturn. By 2015, those same properties had recovered and were worth more than ever.

Cash flow is what separates investors from speculators.

Appreciation Isn't the Goal, But It's the Bonus

Let's say you buy a duplex for $250,000. You put 25% down, finance the rest at 7%, and after all expenses, it cash flows $200 a month. Not life-changing, but solid.

Five years later, the property is worth $320,000. You didn't count on that when you bought it, but the neighborhood improved, rents went up, and demand increased. Now you have options. You could refinance and pull out equity to buy another property. You could sell and redeploy the capital into two smaller deals. Or you could hold it, keep collecting rent, and let the tenant pay down your mortgage.

None of these options existed if you bought purely for appreciation and the property bled cash every month. Cash flow gave you staying power. Appreciation gave you leverage.

Sarah bought her first duplex in 2018 in a mid-sized Midwestern city. She paid $240,000 with 25% down. Each unit rented for $1,100, and after expenses and debt service, the property cash flowed about $250 a month.

She didn't buy it expecting huge appreciation. She bought it because the numbers worked and the neighborhood was stable. Rents were consistent, vacancy was low, and the property was well-maintained.

By 2023, the property was worth $340,000. Rents had increased to $1,350 per unit. Her cash flow had grown to $450 a month, and she had about $100,000 in equity.

She refinanced at a lower rate, pulled out $50,000 in equity, and used that as a down payment on another duplex. The original property still cash flowed $300 a month after the refinance.

In five years, she'd gone from one property to two, without coming out of pocket for the second down payment. The cash flow from the first property gave her stability. The appreciation gave her leverage to scale.

That's how the two work together.

This is the power of buying right from the start. Sarah didn't try to time the market. She didn't bet on gentrification or hope for explosive growth. She bought a property that made financial sense on day one, and the market rewarded her patience with options she hadn't planned for.

Contrast that with investors who bought in the same city but focused solely on appreciation potential. They bought in trendy neighborhoods, paid premium prices, and hoped for rapid value growth. Some succeeded. Many didn't. When the market softened in 2022, those who were over-leveraged and cash-flow-negative had to sell at a loss or subsidize their properties out of pocket.

Sarah, meanwhile, kept collecting her $300 to $450 per month. She had options. She could hold, sell, or refinance. The appreciation was nice, but it wasn't necessary for her strategy to work.

Why "Good Deals" Are Situational

A good deal for one investor might be a terrible deal for another. It depends on what you're trying to accomplish.

Amy is 32, works full-time as a marketing manager, and wants to replace her income in 15 years so she can retire early. She buys properties in stable, affordable markets where rents cover expenses plus $300 per door. She focuses on paying down debt and building equity slowly. She's not trying to scale aggressively. She's building a portfolio of paid-off properties that will generate $4,000 to $5,000 a month by the time she's 47.

For Amy, a good deal is a property that cash flows well and is in a market with low volatility. She doesn't care if it appreciates 2% a year or 8% a year. She cares that it's stable and that she can pay down the mortgage.

Her strategy is boring by design. She's not looking for home runs. She's looking for base hits that compound over time. She buys properties in tertiary markets where prices are affordable and rents are stable. She avoids markets with high growth potential because those same markets tend to have high volatility.

Over ten years, Amy buys six properties. None of them doubled in value. None of them had dramatic rent increases. But all of them cash flowed from day one, and she systematically paid down the mortgages. By year 15, she'll own all six free and clear, generating combined income of $4,500 per month. That's enough to replace her salary and retire.

Amy's friends think she's playing it too safe. They're investing in hot markets, flipping properties, using maximum leverage. Some of them are doing great. Some have already lost money. Amy doesn't care. She's not trying to get rich quick. She's building predictable, reliable income that will free her from her job.

Brian is 28, works as a software engineer, and has access to capital. He wants to build a large portfolio quickly. He buys properties in growing markets, forces appreciation through rehab, refinances to pull his money back out, and repeats. He's leveraged, he's aggressive, and he's banking on equity growth to fund his next move.

For Brian, a good deal is a property he can buy below market, improve, and refinance out of within 12 months. He's not focused on long-term cash flow. He's focused on velocity: how fast he can recycle capital.

Brian's first deal was a single-family home in a growing suburb. He bought it for $180,000, spent $35,000 on rehab, and six months later it appraised for $260,000. He refinanced, pulled out most of his initial investment, and the property cash flowed $150 a month after the new, higher mortgage payment.

That $150 a month isn't much, but Brian didn't buy the property for cash flow. He bought it to recycle capital. He took the money from the refinance and bought another property. Then another. In three years, he owned seven properties using this method.

His portfolio is more leveraged than Amy's. His cash flow is thinner. His risk is higher. But his net worth grew faster because he was able to control more assets with the same amount of capital.

Brian's strategy works because he has a stable, high income from his tech job. If he loses a property to vacancy or a major repair, he can cover it out of pocket. If the market softens and he can't refinance, he has backup plans. His risk tolerance matches his strategy.

Both Amy and Brian are making money. Neither is wrong. The question isn't which strategy is better. The question is which one aligns with your goals, your risk tolerance, and the capital you have available.

The mistake most new investors make is trying to copy someone else's strategy without understanding the context. They see Brian's rapid growth and assume that's what success looks like. Or they see Amy's conservative approach and think she's leaving money on the table. But success is situational. It depends on your age, your income, your risk tolerance, and what you're trying to build.

Time, Leverage, and Patience

Real estate is not a get-rich-quick scheme, but it's one of the most reliable wealth-building tools that exists. The reason is simple: time and leverage.

When you buy a property with a mortgage, your tenant is paying down your debt every month. You're not. They are. Over 15 or 30 years, that adds up. Combine that with inflation, which erodes the real cost of your fixed-rate mortgage, and even modest appreciation, and you're building wealth in three directions at once.

But it requires patience. The first property doesn't change your life. The third one might not either. It's the compounding effect over five, ten, fifteen years that creates financial independence.

Consider this example: You buy a property for $300,000 with a 30-year mortgage at 7%. Your monthly payment is about $1,995. In year one, you pay about $20,800 toward the mortgage, but only $3,200 of that goes to principal. The rest is interest.

That doesn't sound great. But fast forward 10 years. You've paid down about $45,000 in principal. Your tenant paid all of it. You didn't contribute a dollar.

Fast forward 20 years. You've paid down $115,000 in principal. The property is probably worth $450,000 to $500,000, assuming modest 3% annual appreciation. Your equity position is $250,000 or more, and most of it came from your tenant's rent payments and market appreciation, not your pocket.

Now multiply that by five properties.

This is why time matters. The longer you hold, the more powerful the compounding effect becomes.

Let's look at another angle: inflation. If you lock in a 30-year mortgage today at 7%, that rate never changes. But inflation erodes the real cost of that payment every year. A $2,000 mortgage payment today might feel significant. In 20 years, adjusted for inflation, that same $2,000 payment feels like $1,200 in today's dollars.

Meanwhile, rents tend to keep pace with or exceed inflation.

So your income grows while your debt service stays fixed. This creates a widening gap that becomes pure profit over time.

Here's a real example: An investor bought a fourplex in 2003 for $180,000 with a fixed-rate mortgage. His payment was $1,100 per month. In 2003, that felt like a lot. By 2023, that same $1,100 payment felt manageable because his income had doubled and inflation had eroded the real cost.

But rents on that fourplex had grown from $2,800 per month in 2003 to $5,200 per month in 2023. His cash flow went from $400 a month to over $2,500 a month, just by holding the property and letting time work.

The property was also worth $480,000 in 2023. He'd paid down about $80,000 in principal over 20 years. His total equity: $380,000. His tenant paid for almost all of it.

This is the magic of buy-and-hold real estate. You don't need to do anything clever. You just need to buy a property that cash flows, hold it for a long time, and let your tenant build your wealth.

Real estate isn't about getting rich overnight. It's about putting a system in place that works while you sleep, while you work your day job, while you live your life. The property is there, paying for itself, building equity, creating options. You just have to be patient enough to let it work.

The Myth of Passive Income

Let's get one thing straight: real estate is not passive. It's less active than a full-time job, but it's not passive.

You'll get calls about broken water heaters. You'll deal with late-paying tenants. You'll have to make decisions about contractors, leases, and when to raise rents. Even if you hire a property manager, you're still overseeing the operation. You're reviewing financial statements, approving major expenses, and dealing with problems when they escalate.

What real estate offers isn't passive income. It's semi-active income with long-term equity growth. You put in effort upfront, finding deals and securing financing and setting up systems, and ongoing effort managing operations and handling problems. In return, you get monthly cash flow and long-term wealth accumulation.

That's still a great deal. But if you go in expecting to collect checks while you sleep, you'll be disappointed.

For most investors, "passive" means you're not trading time for money in the traditional sense. You're not clocking in at 9am. You're not answering to a boss. Your income isn't capped by your hourly rate or salary.

Instead, you're building systems that generate income with less active involvement over time. You hire property managers. You automate rent collection. You build a team of contractors you trust.

Your first property might take 10 hours a month to manage.

By the time you own five properties with good systems and a property manager, you might spend 5 hours a month overseeing everything.

That's more passive than a W-2 job, but it's not zero effort. It's a business, and businesses require attention.

Here's a realistic breakdown of time commitment:

Self-managing one property: 8 to 12 hours per month. This includes responding to maintenance requests, coordinating with contractors, handling rent collection, and dealing with tenant issues.

Self-managing three properties: 15 to 20 hours per month. You're developing systems at this point, so you're not tripling the time, but you are spending more.

Five properties with a property manager: 5 to 8 hours per month. You're reviewing reports, approving major expenses, and handling escalated issues. The day-to-day is handled.

Ten properties with a property manager and systems: 10 to 15 hours per month. You're spending more time on strategy, acquisitions, and oversight, but less on operations.

Compare that to a full-time job: 160 to 200 hours per month. Real estate isn't passive, but it's dramatically less time-intensive than traditional employment once you have systems in place.

The key is setting expectations correctly. If you go into real estate thinking it's a get-rich-quick, set-it-and-forget-it investment, you'll quit after the first major repair or difficult tenant. If you go in understanding it's a business that requires attention but offers flexibility and long-term wealth creation, you'll stick with it long enough to see results.

Most people who quit real estate do so in the first two years, usually after their first major problem. A tenant trashes the property. A roof needs replacing. An eviction drags on for months. They realize it's not as passive as they thought, and they bail.

The investors who succeed are the ones who knew from the beginning that real estate requires work. They built systems. They hired help when needed. They treated it like a business, not a lottery ticket.

What This Means for You

If you're just starting out, prioritize cash flow. Find properties where the numbers work from day one. Don't buy a property hoping the market will bail you out. Buy properties that make sense today and will make even more sense in five years.

If you already own a few properties and you're looking to scale, start thinking about how appreciation and refinancing can help you grow faster. But don't abandon cash flow in the process. Leverage is powerful, but it's also dangerous if you're over-extended.

And if you're somewhere in the middle, trying to figure out your strategy, remember this: real estate rewards people who think clearly, act deliberately, and stay flexible. The market will change. Your goals will change. Your strategy should change with them.

Define your goals. What are you trying to achieve? Income replacement? Wealth building? Financial freedom? Be specific. Write it down. Review it before every deal.

Decide what matters more to you right now: monthly cash flow or long-term equity growth. You can pursue both, but one will be the priority. That priority will shape which properties you buy and which markets you target.

Build a buy box that reflects those priorities. If cash flow matters most, target markets and properties where rents are strong relative to prices. If appreciation matters most, target growth markets where values are rising.

Remember that you can change your strategy over time. What makes sense at 30 might not make sense at 50. Stay flexible. Reevaluate your goals every few years. Adjust your strategy as your life changes.

The investors who succeed are the ones who understand their own goals clearly enough to build a strategy that supports them. They're not copying what someone else is doing. They're not chasing trends. They're building a portfolio that fits their life, their risk tolerance, and their timeline.

2

Chapter 2: Risk, Return, and Reality

Most people think about risk the wrong way. They treat it like a yes-or-no question: Is this risky or not?

That's not how risk works. Risk is never binary. Every deal carries risk. The question is what kind, how much, and whether you're getting paid enough to take it on.

Risk Is Not Binary

When someone says a deal is "low-risk," what they usually mean is it's familiar. Single-family homes feel less risky than apartment buildings because more people understand them. Properties in your hometown feel safer than properties three states away.

But familiarity isn't the same as safety. A single-family home in a declining market is riskier than a fourplex in a growing one, even if the fourplex feels scarier because it's new to you.

Real risk comes down to a few core factors: Can you cover the mortgage if the property sits vacant? Do you have reserves for unexpected repairs? Is the market stable or volatile? Are you over-leveraged? Can you exit the deal if things go wrong?

Good investors don't avoid risk. They identify it, price it, and decide whether the potential return justifies it.

Let's break down some types of risk you'll encounter:

Market risk: The risk that the market declines and property values drop. This matters most if you need to sell or refinance in the short term. If you're holding long term with strong cash flow, market risk is less relevant because you can wait out downturns.

Vacancy risk: The risk that the property sits empty and you have to cover all expenses out of pocket. This is highest in markets with high vacancy rates or with properties that appeal to a narrow tenant base. A studio apartment in a college town has higher vacancy risk than a three-bedroom house in a family neighborhood.

Maintenance risk: The risk of unexpected, expensive repairs. Older properties carry more maintenance risk. Properties with deferred maintenance carry even more. A property with a 30-year-old roof, original HVAC, and aging plumbing has significant maintenance risk.

Tenant risk: The risk of non-paying tenants, property damage, or legal disputes. This is mitigated through careful screening, but it never goes away entirely. Even good tenants sometimes lose jobs, go through divorces, or fall on hard times.

Financing risk: The risk that interest rates rise, making refinancing more expensive, or that lenders tighten requirements. This matters most if you're using adjustable-rate loans or planning to refinance as part of your strategy.

Concentration risk: The risk of having too much wealth tied up in one property, one neighborhood, or one market. If you own ten properties in the same city and that city's economy tanks, you're in trouble. Diversification reduces this, but it requires more capital.

Regulatory risk: The risk that laws change in ways that hurt landlords. Rent control, eviction moratoriums, new building codes, increased property taxes. These can all impact your returns.

Every property has some combination of these risks. The question isn't whether risk exists. The question is whether you're being compensated for taking it on.

A property with high risk should offer high potential returns. A property with low risk will have lower returns. If you're taking high risk for low returns, you're making a mistake.

How Experienced Investors Underwrite Uncertainty

Here's what separates experienced investors from beginners: they assume things will go wrong.

Beginners underwrite deals at 95% occupancy, minimal repairs, and rents that increase every year. Experienced investors assume 85% occupancy, higher repair costs, and flat rents for the first few years. They stress-test their numbers.

What happens if the roof needs to be replaced in year two? What if interest rates go up and you can't refinance? What if a tenant doesn't pay for three months? If the deal still works under those conditions, it's probably a good deal. If it only works when everything goes perfectly, it's not.

This doesn't mean you need to be paranoid. It means you need to be realistic. Real estate is forgiving if you have margin. It's brutal if you don't.

Here's a practical example of stress testing:

You're analyzing a duplex. The asking price is $280,000. Each unit rents for $1,200. Your projected income is $28,800 per year.

Most beginners stop there. They calculate debt service, subtract fixed expenses, and call it a day.

Experienced investors dig deeper. They ask:

What if vacancy is 15% instead of 5%? That's $4,320 in lost income instead of $1,440. Your net operating income just dropped by $2,880.

What if the HVAC fails in year two? That's $8,000 to $12,000. Do you have reserves to cover it without killing cash flow?

What if a tenant stops paying and it takes four months to evict them? That's $4,800 in lost rent plus legal fees. Can you cover that?

What if rents stay flat for three years instead of growing 3% annually? You just lost $2,500 in projected income growth.

What if property taxes increase 10% next year? That's another $200 to $400 per month in expenses.

What if insurance premiums double due to market conditions? This happened in many markets in 2023 and 2024.

Now run the numbers under these pessimistic assumptions. Does the deal still work? If yes, you have margin. If no, you're speculating.

Margin is what saves you when reality doesn't match your projections. And reality never matches your projections.

An experienced investor looks at that same $280,000 duplex and immediately builds in cushion. They assume:

12% vacancy instead of 5%

$300 per month in maintenance instead of $150

Property taxes increasing 5% every two years

Insurance premiums rising 20% in the next three years

Rents staying flat for the first two years

One major capital expenditure, roof or HVAC, within five years

If the deal still cash flows under those assumptions, they move forward. If not, they pass or negotiate a lower price.

This is why experienced investors can ride out market down-turns while beginners get wiped out. The experienced investors built margin into every deal. When things went wrong, they had room to absorb it.

Why Stability Often Beats Upside

There's a certain type of investor who's always chasing the home run. They want the property that doubles in value in two years. They want the market that's about to explode.

Sometimes they're right. More often, they overpay, over-leverage, and get stuck holding a property they can't afford when the market shifts.

Stability isn't sexy, but it compounds. A property that cash flows $300 a month, every month, for ten years, is worth more than a property that might make you $50,000 if everything goes right but loses money in the meantime.

This is especially true when you're starting out. Your first few properties should be boring. They should work on day one. You'll have plenty of time to take bigger swings once you have a foundation.

Consider two scenarios:

Scenario A: You buy a property in a hot, rapidly growing market. You pay top dollar because competition is fierce. The property barely cash flows, maybe $50 a month, but everyone says the area is booming. You're betting on appreciation.

Two years later, the market softens. New construction floods the area. Rents drop 10%. Your thin cash flow disappears. Now you're subsidizing the property every month, and if you need to sell, you might break even or take a loss after transaction costs.

Scenario B: You buy a property in a stable, boring market. The property cash flows $300 a month from day one. No one's talking about this market. There's no hype. Rents grow slowly, maybe 2% a year. Property values inch up steadily.

Two years later, the market is exactly what you expected: stable. Your cash flow is still $300 a month, maybe $350 now that rents ticked up slightly. You're building equity through principal paydown. You have options.

Scenario B is boring. It won't make for exciting dinner conversation. But over ten years, boring compounds into wealth. Scenario A might work out, but it's a gamble. And when you're building a foundation, you don't want to gamble.

Here's a real example: Two investors bought properties in 2019. Investor A bought in a hot market, paid $400,000, and the property barely cash flowed. Investor B bought in a boring market, paid $200,000, and the property cash flowed $400 a month.

By 2024, Investor A's property was worth $450,000, but still barely cash flowed due to higher expenses and mortgage payments. Total equity: $150,000. Total cash collected over five years: $3,000.

Investor B's property was worth $260,000 and cash flowed $500 a month. Total equity: $120,000 plus $60,000 paid down by tenant. Total cash collected over five years: $24,000.

Both made money, but Investor B had more options and less stress. And if either investor needed to sell in 2024, Investor B could do so easily because their property appealed to both investors and owner-occupants. Investor A's property only appealed to investors willing to accept low cash flow.

Stability wins in the long run.

Personal Risk Tolerance vs. Deal Risk

Not all risk is created equal, and not all investors should take the same risks.

If you're 28, single, and working a stable job, you can afford to be more aggressive. You have time to recover if something goes wrong. If you're 50, supporting a family, and this investment represents a significant portion of your net worth, you need to be more conservative.

Your risk tolerance should inform your strategy, but it shouldn't override the fundamentals. A bad deal is still a bad deal, even if you're young and aggressive. A good deal is still a good deal, even if you're cautious.

The goal is to match your risk tolerance with deal risk in a way that lets you sleep at night while still moving forward.

Here's a framework for assessing your risk tolerance:

Age and time horizon: The younger you are, the more risk you can take. You have time to recover from mistakes. If you're nearing retirement, prioritize stability. A 30-year-old can recover from a failed deal. A 60-year-old might not.

Income stability: If you have a stable W-2 job with steady income, you can handle more risk in your investments. If you're self-employed with variable income, you need more conservative investments that generate predictable cash flow.

Family situation: Supporting a family means you need more predictability. Single with no dependents? You can afford to be more aggressive. Kids in college? You need stability.

Net worth concentration: If this investment represents 50% or more of your net worth, be conservative. If it's 10%, you can take more risk. Never put all your eggs in one basket, especially when you're starting out.

Emergency reserves: Do you have 6 to 12 months of living expenses saved? If yes, you can take more investment risk. If no, build your emergency fund first before investing in real estate.

Personality: Some people genuinely don't stress about volatility. Others lose sleep over every market dip. Know yourself. Don't force a high-risk strategy if it keeps you up at night. The stress isn't worth it.

The worst thing you can do is take on risk that doesn't match your tolerance. You'll make emotional decisions at the worst possible times. You'll sell in a panic. You'll over-leverage because you're chasing returns. You'll sabotage yourself.

Better to earn steady 7% returns while sleeping well than to chase 15% returns while stressing constantly and making bad decisions.

What Good Risk Looks Like

Good risk is calculated. You know what you're getting into, you've stress-tested the numbers, and you have a plan if things don't go as expected.

Good risk is compensated. You're not taking on extra uncertainty for the same return you could get in a safer deal. If the deal is riskier, the potential upside should be higher.

Good risk is manageable. You're not betting everything on one property. You have reserves. You have exit options. You're not over-leveraged to the point where one bad month could sink you.

Bad risk is the opposite. It's impulsive, under-researched, and leaves you with no room for error.

Here's what good risk looks like in practice:

You buy a property that needs moderate rehab. You've inspected it thoroughly. You've got three contractor bids. You've budgeted 20% over the highest bid for contingencies. You have reserves to cover six months of expenses if the rehab runs long. You've stress-tested the post-rehab cash flow under pessimistic assumptions. The numbers still work.

That's good risk. You're taking on uncertainty, the rehab might cost more or take longer, but you've planned for it. You're being compensated for that risk with a below-market purchase price. And you have margin if things go wrong.

Bad risk looks like this:

You buy the same property, but you haven't inspected it. You got one contractor estimate and didn't budget for overruns. You have no reserves. You're counting on refinancing immediately after rehab to pull your money back out. If the rehab goes over budget or takes longer than expected, you're stuck. If the appraisal comes in low, you can't refinance. If the market softens, you're underwater.

Same property, but the second approach is a disaster waiting to happen.

The difference between good risk and bad risk isn't the property. It's the preparation.

Another example of good risk: You buy a property in a market you don't know well, but you've partnered with a local investor who knows the area intimately. You've split the risk. You've learned from someone with experience. You've reduced your exposure.

Bad risk: You buy that same property without a partner, without visiting the market, based purely on numbers from a wholesaler. You have no local knowledge. You can't verify rents or expenses. You're flying blind.

<u>Good risk is informed. Bad risk is blind.</u>

Moving Forward

As you evaluate deals throughout this book, keep coming back to this chapter. Ask yourself: What's the risk here? Am I being compensated for it? Can I handle it if things go wrong?

If the answer to all three is yes, you're probably looking at a good deal. If the answer to any of them is no, walk away.

Real estate rewards patience, discipline, and clear thinking. It punishes greed, sloppiness, and wishful thinking. Know the difference.

Build margin into every deal. Stress-test your assumptions. Match your risk tolerance to your strategy. And never, ever bet more than you can afford to lose.

The investors who survive and thrive are the ones who respect risk without being paralyzed by it. They take calculated risks. They build safety nets. They plan for failure while working toward success.

Be one of those investors.

3

Chapter 3: Deal Analysis Without Overcomplication

Most beginners think deal analysis is complicated. It's not. It's just math, and the math is simpler than you think.

The hard part isn't calculating numbers. The hard part is being honest about them.

What You're Actually Trying to Figure Out

When you analyze a deal, you're answering three questions:

1. Does this property generate enough income to cover all expenses and debt service?

2. Will I get my money back, and if so, how long will it take?

3. What happens if things go wrong?

That's it. Everything else is just different ways of measuring those three things.

Every metric you'll encounter in real estate, cap rate, cash-on-cash return, internal rate of return, debt service coverage ratio, is just a different lens on these same three questions.

The problem is that beginners get overwhelmed by the terminology. They think they need to master complex financial modeling before they can analyze a deal. They don't.

You need to understand a handful of key metrics, be conservative with your assumptions, and stress-test your numbers. That's it.

Let's walk through the metrics that actually matter and ignore the ones that don't.

Cap Rate: What It Tells You, What It Doesn't

Capitalization rate is one of the most misunderstood metrics in real estate. People throw it around like it's gospel, but most of them don't actually know what it means.

Cap rate is net operating income divided by purchase price. It tells you what kind of return you'd get if you bought the property in cash with no financing.

Here's the formula:

Cap Rate = Net Operating Income / Purchase Price

If a property generates $30,000 in NOI and you buy it for $400,000, your cap rate is 7.5%.

So what does that tell you? It tells you how the property performs relative to its price. A higher cap rate usually means higher risk or a less desirable market. A lower cap rate usually means lower risk or a more competitive market.

But cap rate doesn't account for financing, and most investors use financing. So while it's useful for comparing properties in the same market, it's not the whole picture.

Cap rate is most useful for:

Comparing similar properties in the same market. If you're looking at three fourplexes in the same neighborhood, cap rate lets you quickly see which offers the best return relative to price.

Understanding market pricing. If cap rates in a market are compressing, going from 8% to 6%, it means prices are rising faster than income. That might signal you're late to the party.

Commercial real estate valuation. Commercial properties are typically valued based on cap rate, so understanding this metric is essential if you ever move into larger deals.

Cap rate is not useful for:

Evaluating leveraged returns. If you're using a mortgage, your actual return will be different from the cap rate.

Comparing properties in different markets. A 9% cap rate in Detroit isn't directly comparable to a 5% cap rate in San Francisco. Risk profiles are completely different.

Accounting for capital expenditures. Cap rate is based on NOI, which typically doesn't include major capital improvements. A property with a 7% cap rate but a roof that needs replacing soon isn't the same as a property with a 7% cap rate and a new roof.

Use cap rate as one data point among many, not as the definitive measure of whether a deal is good.

Cash-on-Cash Return: The Metric That Actually Matters

If cap rate tells you what happens when you pay cash, cash-on-cash return tells you what happens when you use a mortgage.

Cash-on-cash is annual cash flow divided by the cash you put into the deal.

Cash-on-Cash = Annual Cash Flow / Total Cash Invested

Let's say you buy that same $400,000 property. You put 25% down, so that's $100,000. You also spend $10,000 on closing costs and reserves. Your total cash in is $110,000.

After debt service, the property cash flows $6,000 a year. Your cash-on-cash return is 5.45%.

This is the number you should care about most when you're starting out. It tells you how much cash the property actually generates relative to the cash you have tied up in it.

Cash-on-cash return matters because:

It reflects your actual, leveraged return. This is what you're really earning on the money you invested.

It helps you compare investment options. Is a 5.45% cash-on-cash return better than putting that money in the stock market? In a savings account? In another property?

It highlights the power of leverage. A property with a 6% cap rate might generate a 10% cash-on-cash return if you finance it well.

But here's where beginners get tripped up: they see a 5% or 6% cash-on-cash return and think it's not worth it. They compare it to stock market returns or some guru's promise of 20% returns and decide to pass.

That's a mistake.

Why Cash-on-Cash Gets Misunderstood

People get confused because they think a 5% or 6% cash-on-cash return sounds low. But remember, that's just the cash flow. You're also getting:

Principal paydown: Your tenant is paying off your mortgage every month. On a $300,000 loan at 7%, you're paying down about $3,000 to $4,000 in principal in year one. That's equity you're building without contributing a dollar.

Appreciation: If the property goes up in value, that's additional return. Even modest 3% annual appreciation adds up significantly over time.

Tax benefits: Depreciation and other deductions reduce your taxable income. This isn't cash in your pocket, but it reduces your tax bill, which effectively increases your return.

Inflation hedge: Your fixed-rate mortgage payment stays the same while rents rise with inflation. Over time, this becomes a significant advantage.

When you add all of that together, your total return is much higher than the cash-on-cash number suggests. But cash-on-cash is what you feel in your bank account every month, so it's the number that keeps the property alive.

Let's look at the complete picture with an example:

You buy a $300,000 property with 25% down, $75,000. Your cash-on-cash return is 6%, so you're generating $4,500 in annual cash flow.

But you're also:

Paying down $3,500 in principal in year one. That's equity building.

Benefiting from 3% appreciation, $9,000 in year one. That's equity growth.

Saving $2,000 in taxes due to depreciation and deductions.

Hedging inflation as your mortgage stays fixed but rents rise.

Your total return in year one:

Cash flow: $4,500

Principal paydown: $3,500

Appreciation: $9,000

Tax savings: $2,000

Total: $19,000

That's a 25% return on your $75,000 investment, not 6%.

This is why real estate is such a powerful wealth-building tool. The cash-on-cash return is just one piece of the puzzle.

Rehab Budgeting in Real Terms

If you're buying a property that needs work, your rehab budget can make or break the deal. And most beginners get it wrong.

Here's the rule: whatever you think it's going to cost, add 20%. Not because contractors are dishonest, but because you will find things once you open up walls. You will change your mind about finishes. You will underestimate how long things take.

Get multiple bids. Walk the property with a contractor before you close. Make a line-item budget. Don't just guess.

And remember: rehab costs are part of your total cash invested. If you put $100,000 down and spend $40,000 on rehab, your cash-on-cash calculation is based on $140,000, not $100,000.

Here's a realistic rehab budgeting process:

Inspection: Hire a professional inspector. Get a detailed report. This costs $400 to $600 but saves you thousands by identifying issues early. Don't skip this step.

Contractor walkthrough: Take at least two contractors through the property. Get itemized bids, not just a bottom-line number. You want to see labor, materials, and timeline broken out. Ask questions. Make sure you understand what's included and what's not.

Create a line-item budget: List every item that needs work. Kitchen cabinets, countertops, appliances, flooring, paint, plumbing, electrical, HVAC, roof, landscaping. Price each one separately. This helps you see where money is going and where you might be able to save.

Add contingency: Take your total and multiply by 1.2. That's your real budget. If your line-item budget is $30,000, plan for $36,000. This contingency covers the inevitable surprises: old wiring that doesn't meet code, rotted subfloor under the bathroom, termite damage, etc.

Track spending: As work progresses, track every expense. Use a simple spreadsheet or an app like BuilderTrend. This keeps you aware of where you stand and prevents budget creep. Check in weekly. Review invoices. Make sure work matches what you're being charged for.

Most rehab disasters happen because investors skip these steps. They get a verbal estimate from a contractor, don't put anything in writing, don't budget for contingency, and then act surprised when costs balloon.

Don't be that investor.

Real example: An investor bought a property for $120,000 that needed cosmetic rehab. One contractor bid $15,000. Another bid $22,000. A third bid $18,000. The investor took the $15,000 bid because it was the lowest.

Three weeks into the project, the contractor discovered the electrical panel needed upgrading, $3,000. Then they found water damage under the kitchen sink, $2,500. Then the windows didn't meet egress requirements, $4,000. The investor ended up spending $26,000, nearly double the original bid.

If they'd budgeted conservatively from the start, using the

middle bid of $18,000 plus 20% contingency, they'd have planned for $21,600. They still would have gone over, but not by much. And they wouldn't have been shocked by every surprise.

Always budget conservatively.

Sensitivity Analysis for Normal People

Sensitivity analysis sounds fancy, but it just means asking "what if?"

What if rents are 10% lower than I projected? What if vacancy is 15% instead of 10%? What if I need to replace the HVAC in year two?

Run the numbers under different scenarios. If the deal only works under perfect conditions, it's not a good deal. If it still works when you stress-test it, you're in good shape.

This doesn't require complicated spreadsheets. It just requires honesty and a calculator.

Here's a simple sensitivity analysis process:

Start with your base case: This is your expected scenario. Market rents, normal vacancy, standard expenses. This is what you think will actually happen.

Create a pessimistic case: Drop rents by 10%. Increase vacancy to 15%. Add $3,000 per year for unexpected maintenance.

Increase property taxes and insurance by 10%. Does the deal still cash flow? If not, it's too risky.

Create an optimistic case: Increase rents by 10%. Drop vacancy to 5%. Lower maintenance costs. What's your upside? This helps you understand the best-case scenario, but don't buy based on this. It's gravy, not the reason to buy.

Test major expense scenarios: What if you need a new roof in year three? A new HVAC in year five? A major plumbing repair? Add these costs to your pessimistic case and see if you can still cover debt service. If you can't, you need more reserves or a better deal.

Run the numbers at different exit points: What if you need to sell in year 3 instead of year 10? What if property values drop 10%? Can you still break even or make a small profit? This tells you if you have exit flexibility or if you're locked in.

If your pessimistic case shows negative cash flow, you need more reserves or a better deal. If your base case barely breaks even, the deal is too tight. You want properties that cash flow even when things go wrong.

The goal is to buy properties that work even when things go wrong. Because things will go wrong.

The Numbers Don't Lie, But You Might

The biggest mistake beginners make isn't bad math. It's

convincing themselves the numbers work when they don't.

You want the deal to work, so you round the rent up. You assume low vacancy. You underestimate repairs. You tell yourself the market's about to turn.

Don't do this. If the numbers don't work, the numbers don't work. No amount of optimism will change that. Walk away and find a deal that makes sense from the start.

Here are the most common ways investors lie to themselves:

Optimistic rent projections: You see one comp at $1,400 and three comps at $1,200. You use $1,400 because "your property is nicer." It's not. Use $1,200. Even if your property is nicer, tenants might not pay more. Use conservative numbers.

Low vacancy assumptions: The market average is 10%. You assume 5% because "you'll find great tenants." You might. But plan for 10%. Vacancy is a fact of life. Even the best properties sit empty sometimes.

Ignoring capital expenditures: You budget for maintenance but not for replacing the roof, HVAC, or water heater. These are real costs that will happen. Budget for them. A good rule: set aside 5% of gross rents for CapEx.

Underestimating management: You plan to self-manage, so you don't include property management fees. Then you realize you hate being a landlord and hire a manager. Suddenly your cash flow disappears. Always include management fees in your analysis, even if you plan to manage yourself.

Counting on rent growth: You assume 3% annual rent increases. Maybe that happens. Maybe it doesn't. Underwrite to today's rents and treat growth as a bonus. If the deal doesn't work at current rents, it's not a good deal.

Ignoring market conditions: You assume the market will stay strong. But what if it softens? What if new construction floods the area? What if a major employer leaves town? Build in margin for market changes.

Overestimating your abilities: You think you can do half the rehab work yourself to save money. But you have a full-time job and a family. You won't. Hire professionals and budget accordingly.

The antidote to self-deception is simple: use the worst comp, the highest expense, and the most conservative assumption in every category. If the deal still works, buy it. If not, pass.

This approach will cause you to pass on deals that might have worked out. That's fine. It's better to miss a good deal than to close a bad one.

A Simple Framework

Here's how to analyze a deal in 30 minutes:

1. Pull the rent comps. What are similar units actually renting

for? Use the low end of the range. Look at at least 5 comps. Use only recent comps from the last 3-6 months.

2. Calculate gross income at those rents. Multiply monthly rent by 12. That's your gross potential income.

3. Subtract 10 to 15% for vacancy and credit loss. Even if the property is currently occupied, factor in turnover. Tenants leave. Units sit empty. This is reality.

4. Subtract operating expenses: taxes, insurance, maintenance (budget 1% of property value annually), property management (8-10% of gross rents), utilities you pay, reserves (5% of gross rents for future capital expenditures). Add them all up.

5. What's left is your NOI. This is your net operating income, the income the property generates before debt service.

6. Subtract debt service, your monthly mortgage payment times 12. This is your annual debt service.

7. What's left is your annual cash flow. If this is negative, the deal doesn't work. If it's positive, calculate cash-on-cash return.

8. Divide cash flow by total cash invested (down payment plus closing costs plus any rehab). That's your cash-on-cash return.

If it's 5% or better, and you've been conservative with your numbers, it's probably worth a closer look. If it's below that, move on unless there's a clear plan to improve it through forcing appreciation, reducing expenses, or increasing rents with data to back it up.

This framework works for 90% of deals. It's not perfect, but it's fast and it keeps you from wasting time on properties that don't make sense.

Save the complex financial modeling for after you've bought a few properties and you understand the basics. Start simple. Master this framework first.

Moving Forward

Deal analysis is a skill, and you get better with practice. Run the numbers on properties you're not even buying. Get comfortable with the formulas. Learn what good looks like in your market.

The goal isn't perfection. The goal is clarity. If you can honestly say the numbers work and you've stress-tested them, you're ahead of 90% of investors out there.

Start simple. Master the basics. Get conservative with your assumptions. Stress-test everything. And never, ever convince yourself a bad deal is good just because you want it to work.

The best investors are the ones who can walk away from deals that don't meet their criteria. They're not desperate. They're disciplined. They know another deal will come along.

Be one of those investors.

4

Chapter 4: Where Deals Come From

Everyone wants to know the secret to finding great deals. Here's the truth: there is no secret. Deals come from the same places they've always come from. The difference is consistency, speed, and knowing what you're looking for.

MLS: Why It Still Matters

The MLS gets a bad rap. People act like it's where all the bad deals go, like anything listed publicly has been picked over by smarter investors.

That's not true. Most properties are listed on the MLS because that's where buyers are. Sellers want exposure. Agents want commission. You want inventory. The MLS is still the largest and most reliable source of deals.

Yes, you'll see overpriced properties. Yes, you'll lose out to cash buyers and faster-moving investors. But you'll also find properties that work. Properties where the seller is motivated, the price is fair, and the numbers make sense.

The key is knowing how to filter. Set up alerts for your criteria. Check daily. Be ready to move when something hits. Have your financing lined up so you can close quickly. Speed wins on the MLS.

Here's why the MLS still matters:

Volume: More properties are listed on the MLS than anywhere else. More volume means more opportunities to find something that fits your buy box.

Transparency: MLS listings include detailed information, photos, property history, and days on market. You can see how long a property has been sitting and whether the price has been reduced.

Professional representation: Properties on the MLS have listing agents who can answer questions, schedule showings, and facilitate transactions. This makes the process smoother.

Financing-friendly: Properties on the MLS are easier to finance because lenders are familiar with them. Appraisers can pull comps easily. Inspectors can access the property.

The investors who dismiss the MLS are usually the ones who've never actually bought anything. They're waiting for the perfect off-market deal that never comes. Meanwhile, practical investors are finding perfectly good deals on the MLS every day.

Here's how to use the MLS effectively:

Set up email alerts with specific criteria from your buy box. Property type, price range, location, number of units. You'll get notified the moment something hits the market.

Check listings daily, preferably multiple times per day. Good deals move fast. If you check once a week, you'll always be too late.

Move quickly when you see something that fits. Call your agent immediately. Schedule a showing same day if possible. Make an offer within 24-48 hours if the numbers work.

Be ready to close fast. Have your financing pre-approved. Have your down payment ready. Tell sellers you can close in 21 days or less. Speed is a competitive advantage.

Build relationships with listing agents. If you're professional, responsive, and actually close deals, listing agents will start calling you when they have new listings before they even hit the MLS.

Off-Market: What's Real vs. Exaggerated

Off-market deals sound magical. Everyone wants them. Gurus sell courses on how to find them. But here's what most people don't tell you: off-market deals are harder, slower, and often not as good as they sound.

Off-market just means the property isn't listed. It doesn't mean it's a steal. Most off-market deals come from one of three places:

Direct mail or cold calling: You send letters or make calls to property owners and eventually someone responds. This works, but it takes volume. You might send 1,000 letters to get 10 responses to get 1 deal. And that deal might not even be better than what you'd find on the MLS.

Networking: You meet someone at a real estate meetup, they know someone who wants to sell, you get the introduction. This works too, but it's unpredictable. You can't force it. You have to build genuine relationships over time.

Wholesalers: Someone else found the deal, put it under contract, and is now selling the contract to you for a fee. Sometimes these are great. Often they're overpriced because the wholesaler's fee is baked in. And sometimes the numbers the wholesaler provided are exaggerated.

Off-market deals can work, especially as you scale and build relationships. But they're not where most investors get started, and they're not as consistent as people pretend.

Here's the reality about off-market deals:

They take more time: Finding off-market deals requires con-sistent effort. Direct mail campaigns, in person follow up, networking events, cold calling. This is a part-time job by itself.

They're less transparent: You don't have MLS data, professional photos, or days-on-market information. You're relying on what the seller or wholesaler tells you. Due diligence becomes more important and more difficult.

Financing can be harder: If the property needs significant work or has title issues, lenders might not want to touch it. You might need hard money or cash, which limits your options.

You might not save money: Even if you buy off-market, you're often paying market value or close to it. The seller knows what their property is worth. If they're motivated enough to sell off-market, there's usually a reason, and that reason might mean more work or risk for you.

That said, off-market deals do have advantages:

Less competition: You're not bidding against ten other investors. You can potentially negotiate more directly with the seller.

More flexibility: Without a listing agent and formal process, you can structure creative deals. Seller financing, lease options, subject-to deals. These are easier to negotiate off-market.

Relationship building: Finding off-market deals forces you to build relationships in your market. Those relationships become valuable over time.

If you're just starting out, focus 80% of your effort on the MLS and 20% on building relationships that might lead to off-market deals. As you scale and have more time and resources, you can shift that ratio.

Direct Outreach and Inbound Leads

If you want off-market deals, you need a system. That system is usually some combination of outbound and inbound.

Outbound means you're reaching out: direct mail, cold calling, door knocking, driving for dollars. You're finding properties that look distressed or have motivated sellers, and you're making contact.

Inbound means people are coming to you: you have a website, you run ads, you're active in local groups, and when someone wants to sell, they think of you.

Both take time to build. Both require consistency. And both are hard to justify when you're only looking to buy one or two properties.

If you're starting out, focus on the MLS and your network. Once you own a few properties and you're ready to scale, then invest in direct outreach.

Here's what a direct outreach system looks like:

Identify target properties: Drive neighborhoods looking for

properties that appear distressed. Overgrown lawns, peeling paint, boarded windows. Or use services like PropStream to find lists of properties with high equity, absentee owners, or pre-foreclosure status.

Create messaging: Write a simple letter or script. "Hi, I'm a local investor looking to buy properties in your area. If you're thinking about selling, I'd love to make you an offer. I can close quickly and buy as-is."

Execute consistently: Send 100-200 letters per month or make 50-100 calls per week. Track your responses. Follow up with anyone who shows interest.

Convert leads: When someone responds, ask questions. Why are they selling? What's their timeline? What's the condition of the property? Schedule a walkthrough. Make an offer if the numbers work.

This system requires discipline and consistency. Most people give up after sending one batch of letters or making calls for a week. The investors who succeed are the ones who stick with it for months or years.

Inbound is simpler but takes longer to build:

Create a simple website: "We Buy Houses in [Your City]." Include your contact info, a simple form, and testimonials if you have them.

Run targeted ads: Facebook and Google ads targeting your

market. Budget $500–1,000 per month. Track which ads generate leads.

Be active locally: Join real estate investor groups, attend meetups, comment in local forums. Build your reputation as someone who actually buys properties.

Over time, people will start reaching out to you. But this takes six months to a year of consistent effort before it generates meaningful deal flow.

Why Most "Deal Sources" Dry Up

Here's something no one talks about: most deal sources are temporary.

The wholesaler who sent you three deals last year might not send you any this year. Maybe they left the business. Maybe they found other buyers. Maybe the market changed.

The agent who used to call you first stopped because you didn't close anything. They moved on to investors who actually buy.

The direct mail campaign that worked in 2022 stopped working in 2024 because the market shifted or competition increased.

This is why you can't rely on one source. You need multiple channels. MLS, networking, a good agent relationship, maybe some direct outreach. Diversification isn't just for your portfolio. It's for your deal flow too.

Build relationships with multiple agents. Work with multiple wholesalers. Have multiple marketing channels. That way, when one dries up, you have others producing.

The Real Secret

The real secret to finding deals isn't a magic source. It's this: know what you're looking for, move fast when you find it, and don't waste people's time.

If you've built a clear buy box, you can filter quickly. You're not analyzing every property. You're immediately disqualifying 90% and focusing on the 10% that fit.

If your financing is ready, you can close fast. You're not scrambling to find a lender after you've made an offer. You're pre-approved and ready to go.

If you're professional and responsive, people will bring you deals. Agents want to work with buyers who close. Sellers want to work with buyers who don't waste time. Be that buyer.

Most investors fail at deal sourcing not because they don't know where to look, but because they're slow, indecisive, or unrealistic about what they can afford. Fix that, and deals will find you.

Case Study: Three Deal Sources, Three Different Outcomes

Understanding where deals come from is theoretical until you see it in practice. Here are three real investors who found their first deals through different channels, and what they learned.

Rachel worked with a local real estate agent who specialized in investment properties. She spent three months building the relationship, meeting weekly to review new listings. The agent understood her buy box: duplexes or triplexes in B-class neighborhoods, $200,000 to $280,000, minimum $350 monthly cash flow after all expenses.

The agent sent her 15 properties over three months. Rachel analyzed all 15, made offers on 4, and won 1. The property was a duplex listed at $245,000. She offered $235,000, the seller countered at $240,000, and they settled at $238,000. The property was in good condition, both units were rented at market rates, and it cash flowed $380 per month after all expenses.

Rachel's advantage was the relationship. By the time the right property came on the market, the agent knew exactly what she wanted and called her immediately. She viewed it within hours and made an offer the same day. She wasn't competing against 10 other investors because the agent was filtering opportunities and presenting the best ones to her first.

The downside was time. It took three months of regular communication and analyzing properties before the right one appeared. Many investors give up during this period. Rachel stuck with it because she understood that building relationships takes time.

Marcus went the direct marketing route. He sent 500 letters to out-of-state property owners in his target neighborhoods. The letters were simple: "I'm a local investor looking to buy rental properties in your area. If you're interested in selling, I can make you a fair cash offer with a quick close."

He got 12 responses. Eight were people who wanted retail prices. Two were tire-kickers. Two were legitimate sellers. He made offers on both. One seller accepted.

The property was a triplex owned by someone who inherited it from a parent and lived three states away. They were tired of managing it remotely and dealing with tenant issues. The property was valued around $280,000 but needed $15,000 in deferred maintenance. Marcus offered $250,000 with a 30-day close, all cash. The seller accepted.

After rehab, the property was worth $295,000 and cash flowed $620 per month. Marcus had found a below-market deal because the seller valued speed and certainty over maximum price.

The advantage of direct marketing was control. Marcus didn't wait for properties to hit the MLS. He created his own opportunities. The disadvantage was volume. He sent 500 letters to get one deal. For many investors, that ratio makes direct marketing impractical.

Sophie found her first deal through networking at a local real estate meetup. She attended every month for six months, introduced herself to everyone, and made it clear she was actively looking to buy. At one meetup, she met another investor who was selling a fourplex to fund a larger acquisition.

The fourplex wasn't on the market yet. The seller wanted $310,000. Sophie had it inspected, analyzed the numbers, and offered $295,000. The seller countered at $305,000. They settled at $300,000. The property cash flowed $480 per month and was in excellent condition.

Sophie's advantage was timing. She found the deal before it hit the market, avoiding competition. The disadvantage was that networking takes time and consistent effort. She attended six meetups before finding a deal. Many investors attend once or twice, don't see immediate results, and stop going.

Three different approaches. All three investors found deals. The common thread was persistence and clarity. They knew what they wanted, they were ready to move when opportunities appeared, and they didn't give up after the first few weeks.

Why Speed Matters More Than You Think

In competitive markets, the investor who moves fastest often wins. This doesn't mean making reckless decisions. It means having your systems in place so you can evaluate and act quickly when the right opportunity appears.

Here's what speed actually means in practice:

Pre-approved financing: Before you start looking at properties, get pre-approved for a loan. Not pre-qualified. Pre-approved. This means the lender has reviewed your financials, verified your income, checked your credit, and confirmed you can borrow a specific amount.

When you find a property, you can make an offer with a pre-approval letter the same day. Sellers take these offers seriously. They know you're ready to close.

Investors who wait until after they find a property to start the financing process lose deals. By the time they're approved, someone else has already made an offer.

A clear buy box: When you know exactly what you're looking for, you can evaluate properties in minutes, not days. You look at the listing, check the numbers, and immediately know if it's worth pursuing.

Investors without a buy box waste time analyzing properties that never had a chance of working. They schedule showings for properties outside their price range. They make offers on properties that can't possibly cash flow. They're busy, but they're not productive.

Immediate response time: When an agent or seller contacts you about a property, respond within an hour. If you can't view it that day, schedule it for the next day. If you need to make an offer, do it within 24 hours of viewing.

The investors who take two days to respond, three days to schedule a showing, and a week to decide on an offer lose every competitive deal. The fast investors are already under contract by then.

Systems and checklists: The best investors have checklists for everything. A property evaluation checklist. An inspection checklist. An offer submission checklist. They don't have to remember every step because it's written down.

When a deal appears, they work through the checklist quickly and systematically. Nothing gets forgotten. Nothing slows them down. They're fast because they're organized.

Patience combined with speed sounds contradictory, but it's not. You're patient in waiting for the right deal. You're fast in evaluating and acting when it appears. Most investors get this backward. They're impatient and buy mediocre deals quickly, or they're slow and lose good deals while they deliberate.

The right approach is to wait for quality and pounce when you find it.

Building Multiple Deal Pipelines

Relying on a single deal source is risky. Markets change. Agents move to different brokerages. Wholesalers stop working your area. Direct marketing response rates fluctuate.

The best investors build multiple pipelines so deals flow consistently regardless of which source is active at any given time.

Here's how to build redundancy into your deal sourcing:

Work with three agents: Not one. Three. Each should specialize in different aspects of your market. One focuses on your primary target area. One covers adjacent neighborhoods. One specializes in off-market deals and investor properties. This redundancy means you're always getting deal flow.

If one agent goes quiet, the others pick up the slack. And because they're competing for your business, they're motivated to bring you the best opportunities.

Maintain ongoing direct marketing: Even when you're not actively looking to buy, send 100 to 200 letters per month to potential sellers. This keeps your name in front of people and ensures deal flow when you're ready to buy again.

Direct marketing isn't about immediate results. It's about building a pipeline of future opportunities. Someone who receives your letter today might not be ready to sell for six months. But when they are ready, they'll remember you.

Attend networking events monthly: Real estate meetups, landlord associations, and investor groups are deal pipelines disguised as social events. The deals don't appear the first time you attend. They appear after you've become a familiar face and people know you're serious.

Go to the same events consistently. Introduce yourself to new people every time. Follow up with the people you meet. Over time, you'll build a network that brings you off-market deals, partnership opportunities, and industry intelligence.

Monitor the MLS daily: Even if you have agents searching for you, set up your own MLS alerts. This keeps you informed about market trends, pricing, and competition. It also helps you spot deals your agents might have missed.

You don't need to analyze every listing. Just scan them daily to stay current. When something interesting appears, reach out to your agent immediately.

Stay active in online communities: BiggerPockets, local Facebook groups, and market-specific forums are places where deals occasionally appear. More importantly, they're places where you can learn about market trends, find contractors, and connect with other investors.

The goal isn't to spend hours on these platforms. It's to check in regularly, contribute value, and stay visible so opportunities come to you.

The investors who struggle to find deals are usually doing one thing. They're working with one agent or trying one marketing channel. When that channel slows down, they have nothing else. Their deal flow stops completely.

The investors who consistently find deals are doing five to ten things. Not all of them produce deals all the time, but enough of them are active that deal flow stays consistent.

When to Stop Looking and When to Keep Searching

One of the hardest skills for new investors is knowing when a property is good enough to buy and when to keep searching. This judgment comes with experience, but here are some guidelines.

Stop looking and make an offer when:

The property fits your buy box and the numbers work: If it meets all your criteria and cash flows at your target level, make an offer. Don't wait for a perfect property. Perfect doesn't exist.

The property is better than what you've seen in the past 30 days: If this is the best opportunity you've seen recently, it's probably a good deal. Market conditions don't change overnight. If nothing better has appeared in a month, nothing better is likely to appear tomorrow.

You can close quickly and with certainty: If you're pre-approved, have reserves, and can close on the seller's timeline, you have a competitive advantage. Use it. Quick, certain buyers win deals.

Keep searching when:

The property doesn't fit your buy box: Don't compromise on your core criteria just because you're tired of looking. If it's the wrong property type, wrong neighborhood, or wrong price range, keep searching.

The numbers are close but not quite there: "Close" doesn't count in real estate. If the property needs to appreciate 10% to make sense, or if cash flow depends on rents increasing immediately, walk away. Wait for a deal that works on day one.

You're buying out of fear or impatience: If you're making an offer because you're worried you'll never find another deal, stop. That's fear, not analysis. The right deal will appear. It always does if you're patient and persistent.

You haven't seen enough properties: If you've only looked at five properties, you probably don't know your market well enough yet. Keep analyzing deals until you've seen at least 20 to 30. By then, you'll have a feel for what's normal and what's exceptional.

The key is to stay objective. Don't fall in love with properties. Don't make offers just to make offers. But also don't wait for perfection. The best investors find the balance between patience and action.

Building Your Network for Deal Flow

The most successful investors aren't just good at finding properties. They're good at building relationships that bring properties to them. This takes time, but it compounds.

Start by joining your local real estate investor association. Most cities have monthly meetups where investors share deals, strategies, and resources. Show up consistently. Don't be the person who shows up once, pitches everyone on your deal, and disappears. Be the person who adds value, shares knowledge, and builds genuine relationships.

Attend at least six meetings before you expect anything in return. Listen more than you talk. Ask questions. Take notes. When someone mentions a problem, think about how you can help solve it, even if it doesn't directly benefit you.

Over time, you'll become known in your market. Wholesalers will start sending you deals. Agents will call you when they have off-market opportunities. Other investors will refer properties that don't fit their criteria but might fit yours.

This doesn't happen overnight. It takes 6 to 12 months of con-sistent showing up. But once you've built these relationships, they become one of your most valuable assets.

Real example: An investor started attending his local REIA in 2019. For the first six months, he just listened and learned. He didn't buy anything. He didn't pitch anyone. He just showed up and built relationships.

By month 8, a wholesaler approached him with an off-market duplex. The numbers worked. He bought it. Over the next three years, that same wholesaler sent him four more deals, all of which he purchased.

Those five properties came from one relationship that started by simply showing up consistently to a monthly meeting.

Network building isn't glamorous, but it works.

5

Chapter 5: Building Your Buy Box

Before you start looking at properties, you need to know what you're looking for. This is called a buy box, and it's one of the most important tools you'll build as an investor.

A buy box is a clear, specific set of criteria that defines what properties you'll consider and what you won't. It keeps you focused, saves time, and prevents you from chasing deals that don't fit your strategy.

Why Most Investors Skip This Step

Most beginners don't build a buy box. They just start looking at properties and hope something jumps out. This leads to analysis paralysis, wasted time, and bad decisions made out of frustration.

Without a buy box, every property looks interesting. You spend hours analyzing deals that were never going to work. You get excited about properties outside your price range or in markets you don't understand. You make emotional decisions because you're tired of looking and just want to buy something.

With a buy box, you can disqualify 90% of properties in 30 seconds and focus your energy on the 10% that actually matter.

A buy box is your filter. It's how you stay disciplined when every guru is telling you about the next hot market or the next can't-miss strategy.

What Goes Into a Buy Box

Your buy box should include:

Geography: What markets or neighborhoods are you targeting? Be specific. Don't just say "Phoenix." Say "West Phoenix, within 10 miles of downtown, near public transit." Or "East Nashville within 5 miles of downtown."

The more specific you are, the better. You want to know your target area well enough to identify good and bad streets, understand school districts, and recognize value.

Property type: Single-family? Duplex? Fourplex? Small multifamily? Each has trade-offs. Pick one to start. Don't try to analyze single-family homes, apartment buildings, and commercial properties all at once. Master one property type, then expand.

Price range: What can you afford? What price point gives you the best cash-on-cash return in your market? Be realistic. If you can afford $300,000, don't waste time looking at $500,000 properties.

Condition: Are you looking for turnkey properties, light rehab, or heavy value-add? Be honest about your skills, time, and capital. If you work full-time and have no construction experience, turnkey is probably your best bet.

Minimum cash flow: What's the lowest monthly cash flow you'll accept? For most investors starting out, $200 per door per month is a reasonable floor. Some investors set it higher, $300 or $400 per door. This ensures the property generates meaningful income.

Minimum cash-on-cash return: What return justifies tying up your capital? 5%? 7%? 10%? This will vary by market and strategy. In expensive markets, 5% might be acceptable. In cheaper markets, you might demand 8% or more.

Occupancy: Are you willing to buy vacant properties, or do you want tenants in place? Vacant means you have to find tenants and start cash flow from scratch. Occupied means you inherit existing tenants, which could be good or bad.

Financing: Are you using conventional loans? DSCR? Cash? Your financing options will limit your property options. Conventional loans max out at 10 properties. DSCR loans work for more but cost more. Know your financing constraints.

How to Build Your Buy Box

Start by asking yourself three questions:

1. What are my goals? Income replacement? Portfolio growth? Wealth building over 20 years? Be specific. "I want to replace $5,000 per month of income in 10 years" is better than "I want financial freedom."

2. What capital do I have? How much can I put down? How much do I need in reserves? If you have $75,000, that's your limit. Don't fantasize about $200,000 deals.

3. What markets or neighborhoods do I know well enough to invest in? Start where you have knowledge. Your hometown. A city where you went to college. A market where you have family or friends. Local knowledge is a massive advantage.

Then research your target market. Look at comparable properties on the MLS. What are they renting for? What are they selling for? What kind of returns are realistic?

Talk to local agents. Ask what's selling. Ask about rental rates. Ask about vacancy. Get real data, not guesses.

Once you have that data, you can build a buy box that's grounded in reality, not fantasy.

An Example Buy Box

Here's what a buy box might look like for a first-time investor:

Geography: East Nashville, within 5 miles of downtown, east of the interstate, south of Dickerson Pike

Property type: Duplex or small multifamily, 2 to 4 units

Price range: $300,000 to $450,000

Condition: Turnkey or light cosmetic rehab, under $20,000 in repairs

Minimum cash flow: $300 per month after all expenses

Minimum cash-on-cash return: 6%

Occupancy: Prefer tenants in place, will consider vacant if priced right

Financing: Conventional loan, 25% down, 30-year fixed

With this buy box, you can evaluate properties quickly. If it's outside East Nashville, it's a no. If it's over $450,000, it's a no. If it needs major rehab, it's a no. If it cash flows under $300, it's a no.

You don't need to waste time running full analysis on properties that were never going to work. You filter first, analyze second.

Your Buy Box Will Evolve

Your first buy box won't be perfect, and that's fine. You'll learn as you go. Maybe you realize the neighborhoods you targeted are too expensive. Maybe you find that duplexes are harder to finance than you thought. Maybe your cash flow target was unrealistic for your market.

That's all normal. Adjust your buy box as you learn more. The point isn't to get it perfect on day one. The point is to have a filter that keeps you focused and prevents you from chasing every shiny object that crosses your path.

After you buy your first property, revisit your buy box. What worked? What didn't? What would you change? Update it and move forward.

Your buy box should evolve as you gain experience, as markets change, and as your goals shift. It's a living document, not a tattoo.

Share Your Buy Box

Once you have a buy box, share it. Tell your agent. Tell your network. Post it in investor groups. The clearer you are about what you're looking for, the more likely people are to bring you deals that actually fit.

Most investors are vague. They say "I'm looking for cash-flowing properties." That's not helpful. Every investor wants cash-flowing properties.

If you say "I'm looking for duplexes in East Nashville, $300K to $450K, turnkey or light rehab, need to cash flow at least $300 a month," people can actually help you. An agent hears that and thinks, "I have something that might work." A wholesaler hears that and knows whether to send you deals.

Specificity attracts deals. Vagueness repels them.

Moving Forward

Before you look at another property, build your buy box. Write it down. Make it specific. Then use it to filter everything you see.

It will save you time, keep you disciplined, and dramatically increase your chances of finding a deal that actually works.

And when people tell you about deals outside your buy box, politely pass. Stay focused. Trust your criteria. Wait for properties that fit.

The investors who succeed are the ones who know what they're looking for and have the discipline to wait for it.

Using Data to Refine Your Buy Box

Your initial buy box will be based on research and assumptions. As you analyze deals and talk to people in your market, you'll gather data that helps you refine it.

Track every property you analyze, even the ones you don't buy. Create a simple spreadsheet with columns for: address, asking price, estimated rent, estimated expenses, estimated cash flow, and why you passed or made an offer.

After analyzing 20 to 30 properties, patterns will emerge. You'll see that certain neighborhoods consistently have better rent-to-price ratios. You'll notice that properties in a certain price range always need more work than you're comfortable with. You'll discover that your cash flow target was too aggressive or too conservative.

Use this data to update your buy box. Maybe you started targeting fourplexes but discovered that duplexes in your market have better returns. Maybe you started looking at properties up to $400,000 but found that the sweet spot is actually $280,000 to $350,000.

This iterative process of analyze, learn, adjust is how you develop an accurate buy box that actually reflects your market, not just your hopes.

Most investors skip this step. They create a buy box, never update it, and wonder why they can't find deals. The investors who succeed are the ones who treat their buy box as a living document that evolves as they learn.

Geographic Specificity Matters More Than You Think

When defining your target geography, the more specific you

can be, the better. Don't just say "Kansas City." Say "the Waldo neighborhood and the areas within half a mile of Troost Avenue between 50th and 70th Street."

Why does this matter? Because real estate is hyperlocal. Two streets can have completely different dynamics. One side of a major road can be appreciating while the other side is declining.

The more specific your geography, the more you can develop expertise. You'll learn which streets are good and which to avoid. You'll recognize when a property is overpriced or underpriced based on the exact location. You'll build relationships with agents who specialize in that area.

This level of specificity also helps when you're networking. If you tell an agent "I'm looking anywhere in Nashville," they can't help you. There are hundreds of neighborhoods. If you say "I'm focused on East Nashville, specifically the Lockeland Springs and Five Points areas," they immediately know whether they have something for you.

Start narrow. Master one neighborhood or zip code. Then expand from there. Don't try to cover an entire city when you're just starting out.

6

Chapter 6: Understanding Market Cycles

Real estate moves in cycles. Prices go up, prices go down, sometimes they sit still for years. If you're going to invest successfully over the long term, you need to understand these cycles and adjust your strategy accordingly.

The good news: you don't need to time the market perfectly. You just need to avoid doing something catastrophically stupid at the wrong time.

The Four Phases

Markets move through four general phases:

Expansion: Prices are rising, demand is strong, inventory is low. Buyers compete for properties. Rents increase. New construction starts. This is when most people want to invest, which ironically is when you need to be most careful.

Peak: Prices have gotten expensive. Buyers start hesitating. Some investors start exiting. Inventory might tick up slightly, but transactions are still happening. This is the hardest phase to identify in real time because optimism is still high.

Contraction: Prices fall or flatten. Demand softens. Inventory builds. Sellers who bought recently start panicking. Investors who over-leveraged start getting squeezed. This is when most people stop investing, which is often the wrong move.

Bottom: Prices have stabilized at a new, lower level. Fear dominates sentiment. Inventory is higher but transactions are slower because buyers are scared. This is actually when the best deals happen, but it doesn't feel like it. Fear keeps most people on the sidelines.

Then the cycle starts again.

Understanding where you are in the cycle helps you adjust your strategy. You don't need to predict the future. You just need to recognize the present.

Why Timing Matters Less Than Structure

Here's what most people get wrong: they think the goal is to buy at the bottom and sell at the peak. That's not realistic. You can't time it that precisely, and trying to will just keep you on the sidelines.

What matters more is the structure of your deal. If you buy a property with strong cash flow, conservative leverage, and a long-term hold strategy, you can buy at almost any point in the cycle and still do fine. The property pays for itself while you wait for appreciation.

If you buy a property with no cash flow, maximum leverage, and a plan to flip it in 12 months, you better hope the market keeps going up. If it doesn't, you're in trouble.

Structure protects you from bad timing. Speculation doesn't.

An investor bought a fourplex in 2006, right before the crash. Terrible timing. But the property cash flowed $600 per month. When the market crashed in 2008, values dropped 30%. But the investor didn't care because they weren't selling. They kept collecting rent. By 2015, the property had recovered. By 2023, it was worth 50% more than they paid.

Another investor bought a condo in 2006 as a flip. No cash flow, maximum leverage, planned to sell in six months. The market crashed. They couldn't sell. They couldn't afford the mortgage. They lost the property to foreclosure.

Same market, same timing, different outcomes. The difference was structure.

How to Avoid Buying Into Hype

Every market has a moment when prices seem to defy gravity.

Everyone's buying. Agents are breathless. Investors are waiving inspections and bidding over ask. It feels like you're going to miss out if you don't act now.

This is exactly when you need to slow down.

Hype is expensive. When everyone wants in, prices overshoot fundamentals. Rents might not support the purchase price. Cap rates compress to levels that don't make sense. You end up paying for future appreciation that might not happen.

The antidote to hype is boring discipline. Go back to your numbers. If the cash flow doesn't work, walk away. If you have to make aggressive assumptions to justify the price, walk away. There will always be another deal.

Signs you're buying into hype:

Everyone's talking about this market or neighborhood. If your barber and your dentist are all talking about real estate, you're probably late.

Prices are rising faster than rents. If property values are up 15% but rents are only up 3%, the math may not work.

Investors are waiving contingencies to compete. If people are skipping inspections, that's desperation, not confidence.

Projected returns rely on appreciation. If the only way the deal works is if prices keep rising, you're speculating.

New construction is everywhere. Cranes in the sky mean supply is coming. More supply means competition for tenants and downward pressure on rents.

When you see these signs, be cautious. Tighten your underwriting. Demand better cash flow. Or wait.

Long-Term vs. Short-Term Thinking

Short-term investors, flippers, and speculators care a lot about market cycles. They're trying to get in and out before the market shifts. If they're wrong, they lose.

Long-term investors care less. They're buying properties that generate income today and will keep generating income in five years, ten years, twenty years. If prices go up, great. If prices go down, it doesn't matter because they're not selling.

This is one reason cash flow is so important. Cash flow gives you time. You're not forced to sell in a down market. You can wait it out.

The investors who got wiped out in 2008 were the ones who needed prices to keep rising. The investors who survived and thrived were the ones whose properties paid for themselves.

Adjusting Your Strategy to the Cycle

You don't need to sit out entire phases of the market. You just need to adjust your strategy.

Early expansion: This is when appreciation plays start to make sense. Markets are recovering, prices are rising, and you can benefit from equity growth. Just make sure the cash flow still works. Don't abandon fundamentals just because the market's moving.

Late expansion / peak: Be more conservative. Tighten your underwriting. Look for value-add opportunities where you can force appreciation instead of relying on the market. Consider taking some chips off the table if you have properties that have appreciated significantly. Maybe refinance and pull out equity. Maybe sell and take profits.

Contraction: Focus on cash flow and stability. Look for motivated sellers. Be ready to move when others are scared. This is when patient investors with capital can find great deals. Don't try to catch a falling knife, but watch for stabilization.

Bottom: Buy aggressively if you have the capital. Everyone else is sitting on the sidelines, which means less competition and better prices. Just make sure the fundamentals are sound. Don't buy just because it's cheap. Buy because the numbers work.

The Long Game

If you're building a portfolio over 10, 15, 20 years, you're going to see multiple cycles. Prices will go up. Prices will go down. Markets will boom. Markets will crash.

None of that matters if you buy properties that generate income, manage them well, and hold them long enough for compounding to work.

The investors who get hurt are the ones who over-leverage, over-pay, and assume the market will bail them out. The investors who win are the ones who buy smart, stay disciplined, and give time a chance to work.

7

Chapter 7: Financing Investment Property

How you finance a property is just as important as which property you buy. The wrong loan can turn a good deal into a bad one. The right loan can make a marginal deal work.

Most beginners don't spend enough time thinking about financing. They assume there's one way to do it, take whatever their lender offers, and move forward. That's a mistake.

Conventional Loans: The Default Option

For most investors buying their first few properties, a conventional loan is the best option. These are mortgages backed by Fannie Mae or Freddie Mac. They offer competitive rates, long terms usually 30 years, and relatively straightforward approval.

To qualify, you'll need:

A down payment of at least 10 to 25%. Investment properties require more than primary residences.

Good credit, starting around 620+ but usually 680 or higher, though 720+ gets better rates.

Proof of income through W-2s, tax returns, or pay stubs.

Debt-to-income ratio under a certain threshold, usually 43 to 50%.

Cash reserves, usually 6 months of payments on all properties you own.

Conventional loans are great because they're cheap, relatively low interest rates compared to other options, predictable with fixed-rate options available, and scalable. You can have up to 10 of them.

The downside: they're strict about income documentation and debt ratios, which can be limiting if you're self-employed or if your income is complicated.

DSCR Loans: Explained Clearly

DSCR stands for Debt Service Coverage Ratio. These are loans designed specifically for investors, and they work differently than conventional loans.

Instead of looking at your personal income, DSCR loans look

at the property's income. The lender calculates whether the property generates enough rent to cover the mortgage payment. If it does, you qualify.

The formula is simple:

DSCR = Net Operating Income / Annual Debt Service

If the property generates $24,000 in NOI and the mortgage costs $20,000 a year, your DSCR is 1.2. Most lenders want to see a DSCR of at least 1.0, though some require 1.1 or 1.25.

The advantage of DSCR loans: they don't care about your personal income. If you're self-employed, have complicated tax returns, or already own multiple properties that consume your debt-to-income ratio, DSCR loans can be easier to qualify for.

The downside: they're more expensive. Interest rates are typically 1 to 2% higher than conventional loans, and fees can be higher too.

When does a DSCR loan make sense? When you can't qualify for a conventional loan, when the property cash flows well enough to justify the higher rate, or when speed matters and you need to close fast.

Hard Money: When It Actually Makes Sense

Hard money loans are short-term, high-interest loans secured by the property. They're expensive, rates can be 10 to 15%, and they come with fees, 2 to 5 points upfront, but they're fast and flexible.

Most investors hear "hard money" and assume it's predatory. It's not. It's just a different tool for a different situation.

Hard money makes sense when:

You're buying a property that needs significant rehab and won't qualify for traditional financing.

You need to close quickly. Hard money can fund in days, not weeks.

You plan to refinance into a conventional loan once the rehab is done.

Hard money does not make sense for buy-and-hold properties you plan to keep long-term. The rates are too high. You'll eat through your cash flow just covering the interest.

Think of hard money as bridge financing. You use it to buy and fix a property, then you refinance into cheaper, long-term debt. If you can't refinance out of it within 12 to 18 months, you probably shouldn't be using hard money in the first place.

Creative Financing: Benefits and Dangers

Creative financing is a catch-all term for anything that's not a traditional mortgage. Seller financing, subject-to deals, lease options, private money, partnerships: all of these fall under creative financing.

These strategies can work, especially in markets where traditional financing is hard to come by or when you're dealing with motivated sellers. But they come with risks.

Seller financing: The seller acts as the bank. You make payments directly to them instead of a lender. This can be great if the seller owns the property free and clear and is willing to carry a note. The risk: if the seller has their own mortgage, you might be violating their due-on-sale clause, which could trigger a loan call.

Subject-to: You buy the property but leave the seller's existing mortgage in place. You take over the payments, but the loan stays in their name. This can work in specific situations, but it's legally complex and risky for both parties.

Private money: You borrow from an individual investor instead of a bank. This can be faster and more flexible, but it's also more expensive and requires strong relationships.

Creative financing is not inherently bad, but it's not a replacement for understanding traditional financing. Learn conventional and DSCR loans first. Once you understand those, you can layer in creative strategies where they make sense.

How Much Leverage Is Too Much?

Leverage is powerful. It lets you control a $400,000 property with $100,000. It magnifies your returns. But it also magnifies your risk.

The more leveraged you are, the less margin for error you have. If the property sits vacant for a few months, can you cover the mortgage? If rents drop 10%, does the cash flow disappear? If you need to sell, can you do so without bringing cash to closing?

Conservative investors aim for a debt-to-equity ratio of 70 to 80%. That means if you own a $400,000 property, you have at least $80,000 to $120,000 in equity. This gives you cushion.

Aggressive investors push 90% leverage or higher. This maximizes returns when things go well, but it also increases the risk of foreclosure or forced sales when things go wrong.

There's no universal right answer. It depends on your risk tolerance, your reserves, and your goals. Just know that more leverage means more risk, and plan accordingly.

A Simple Financing Strategy

For most investors starting out, here's a simple approach:

Use conventional loans for your first few properties. They're cheap, predictable, and scalable.

Once you hit the limit on conventional loans, usually up to 10 properties, (depends on reserves and financials) start using DSCR loans, non qm, business purpose loans for additional purchases.

Use hard money only for properties that need rehab and that you plan to refinance within 12 months.

Avoid creative financing until you understand traditional financing inside and out.

Financing is a tool. The goal is to match the right tool to the right situation, not to use the most complex or exotic option available.

8

Chapter 8: Property Type Decisions

Not all properties are created equal. Single-family homes, duplexes, fourplexes, small apartment buildings: each has different risk profiles, management demands, and financial characteristics.

Choosing the right property type for your first few investments is one of the most important decisions you'll make.

Single-Family vs. Multifamily

This is the first big fork in the road. Do you start with single-family homes or do you jump straight into multifamily?

Single-family homes are easier to finance, easier to sell, and easier to understand. Most people have lived in a single-family home, so the concept is familiar. Banks love them. Buyers love them. If you need to exit, you can sell to an owner-occupant, not just another investor.

The downside: single-family homes offer limited scalability. One property, one tenant, one income stream. If that tenant leaves, you're at zero. And because the property only has one unit, your cash flow per property is usually lower than multifamily.

Multifamily properties, duplexes, triplexes, fourplexes, offer better cash flow per property and built-in diversification. If one unit is vacant, the others are still generating income. You can also spread fixed costs like property management, insurance, and maintenance across multiple units, which improves your margins.

The downside: multifamily properties are harder to finance, especially once you go beyond fourplexes, harder to manage, and harder to sell. Your buyer pool is mostly other investors, not owner-occupants.

So which should you choose?

If you want simplicity, lower risk, and easier financing, start with single-family or duplexes. If you want faster scaling and better cash flow per property, start with triplexes or fourplexes.

There's no wrong answer. It depends on your goals and your market. Just don't overthink it. Most investors do fine with either path.

Vacancy and Concentration Risk

Concentration risk is the risk of having too much of your wealth tied up in one asset or one market. It's one of the biggest risks new investors underestimate.

If you own one single-family home and the tenant leaves, you go from 100% occupancy to 0% overnight. If you own a fourplex and one tenant leaves, you drop from 100% to 75%. The fourplex is more resilient.

This is one of the main arguments for multifamily. But it cuts both ways. If you own four single-family homes in different neighborhoods and one tenant leaves, you're still at 75% occupied across your portfolio. Same result, different structure.

The point isn't that one is better. The point is that concentration risk exists no matter what you buy. The solution is diversification: multiple properties, multiple neighborhoods, ideally multiple markets.

But when you're starting out, diversification is expensive. You probably can't afford to buy four properties in four markets. So you do the best you can with the capital you have, and you acknowledge the risk.

Management Intensity

Single-family homes are easier to manage than multifamily. One tenant, one lease, one set of problems. Multifamily means multiple leases, multiple tenants, and more things that can go wrong at the same time.

That said, multifamily is often more efficient to manage once you have systems in place. You can visit one property and handle issues for four units instead of driving to four different houses. If you hire a property manager, the cost per unit is usually lower for multifamily.

So yes, multifamily is more intense. But it's also more scalable.

Exit Flexibility

Single-family homes are easier to sell. Your buyer pool includes owner-occupants, which is a much larger market than investors. If you need to exit quickly, single-family is your best bet.

Multifamily properties have a smaller buyer pool. You're mostly selling to other investors, and those investors will analyze the numbers closely. If the property doesn't cash flow well, you might struggle to find a buyer at your asking price.

This is something to think about before you buy. If there's any chance you'll need to sell in the next few years, single-family gives you more options.

What to Start With

If you're brand new and buying your first property, here's a simple framework:

If you want simplicity and lower risk: single-family home

If you want better cash flow and some diversification: duplex or triplex

If you're willing to take on more complexity for better returns: fourplex

Whatever you choose, make sure it fits your buy box, cash flows from day one, and is in a market you understand. Property type matters, but it's not as important as the fundamentals.

9

Chapter 9: Managing Property Like a Business

Owning rental property is not passive. It's a business. And like any business, it requires systems, discipline, and consistent execution.

Most new investors underestimate this. They think once they buy the property, the hard part is over. It's not. The hard part is managing it well for the next 10, 20, 30 years.

Tenant Selection Principles

Your tenant is your customer. Pick the wrong customer, and you'll spend the next year dealing with late payments, property damage, and legal headaches. Pick the right customer, and the property practically manages itself.

Here's what good tenant selection looks like:

Credit check: Look for a history of paying bills on time. A credit score isn't everything, but it's a useful signal. If someone has a 500 credit score and three evictions, that's a red flag.

Income verification: The standard rule is the tenant's gross monthly income should be at least 3x the rent. If rent is $1,500, they should make at least $4,500 a month. Get pay stubs or bank statements.

Rental history: Call previous landlords. Ask if the tenant paid on time, caused damage, and left the property in good condition. If a landlord is evasive or won't give a reference, that's a red flag.

Background check: Run a criminal background check. You're not necessarily disqualifying someone for having a record, but you need to know what you're getting into.

Meet them in person: Trust your gut. If something feels off, it probably is.

The goal isn't to find the perfect tenant. The goal is to avoid the bad ones. Most tenants are fine. A small percentage will make your life miserable. Screen carefully and you'll filter out most of the problems before they start.

Systems, Not Personalities

A lot of landlords run their properties like a hobby. They manage by feel. They make exceptions. They let things slide because they like the tenant or feel bad or don't want to deal with conflict.

This doesn't scale, and it leads to problems.

The solution is systems. Have a written lease. Have written policies. Enforce them consistently. No exceptions.

Late payments: Charge a late fee. Every time. If rent is due on the 1st and it's not paid by the 5th, start the eviction process. This sounds harsh, but it's not. It's professional.

Maintenance requests: Have a system for tenants to submit requests. Respond within 24 hours. Fix urgent issues immediately. Schedule non-urgent issues within a reasonable timeframe. Document everything.

Move-in and move-out inspections: Use a checklist. Take photos. Make the tenant sign off. This protects you from bogus damage claims later.

Lease renewals: Give tenants 60 to 90 days notice before the lease expires. If you're raising rent, explain why. If they're good tenants, consider keeping the increase modest to avoid turnover.

Systems reduce conflict, protect you legally, and make the business predictable. They're not sexy, but they work.

Dealing With Difficult Tenants

Even with great screening, you'll eventually deal with a difficult tenant. Here's how to handle common situations:

The Late Payer: They're always a few days late with rent. They have excuses every month. This will drain your energy and create cash flow problems.

Solution: Enforce your late fees consistently. After the second late payment, have a conversation about whether the property is still affordable for them. After the third, start the eviction process. Sounds harsh, but chronic late payment is a sign they can't afford the property. Better to help them transition out now than to have an eviction on both your records six months from now.

The Excessive Maintenance Requester: They call about every little thing. The faucet drips. The door squeaks. The light bulb needs changing.

Solution: Set clear expectations in the lease about what's their responsibility and what's yours. Provide a maintenance request portal so all requests are documented. Respond professionally but don't drop everything for non-urgent issues. Group non-urgent work orders to minimize trips and contractor costs.

The Problem Neighbor: Other tenants or neighbors complain about noise, parties, or behavior.

Solution: Document every complaint. Send written warnings. Reference the lease clauses they're violating. If behavior continues, start eviction proceedings. You can't let one bad tenant ruin the property for everyone else.

The Messy Tenant: The property is clean when you inspect, but you hear from neighbors or see from outside that it's not being maintained.

Solution: Regular inspections, allowed by most leases with proper notice, typically 24 to 48 hours. Document issues with photos. Send written notices requiring correction within a specific timeframe. If they don't comply, you may have grounds to terminate the lease depending on your state laws.

In all cases, document everything. Keep records of every conversation, text, email, and notice. If you end up in court, documentation is everything.

Creating Tenant Retention Programs

Turnover is expensive. Every time a tenant leaves, you pay for cleaning, repairs, marketing, showings, screening, and vacancy. It can easily cost $2,000 to $4,000 per turnover.

That's why retaining good tenants is one of the best investments you can make. Here's how:

Annual lease renewal bonuses: Offer tenants a small rent discount or a one-time $200 gift card if they renew their lease 60 days before expiration. It's cheaper than turnover and locks in occupancy.

Responsive maintenance: Fix issues quickly. Tenants who feel taken care of are more likely to stay.

Modest rent increases: If you have a great tenant, consider raising rent by only 2 to 3% annually instead of 5 to 7%. The extra $30 to $50 per month you might have gotten isn't worth losing a good tenant.

Seasonal touches: Send a small gift during the holidays. A $25 gift card with a thank-you note goes a long way toward making tenants feel valued.

Quick lease renewal offers: Contact tenants 90 days before lease expiration. Make it easy for them to renew. Provide the new lease immediately. The longer they have to think about moving, the more likely they are to explore other options.

These strategies cost very little and dramatically reduce turnover. Reducing turnover by even one tenant per year across a small portfolio can save $5,000 to $10,000 annually.

Maintenance Planning

Maintenance comes in three flavors: **preventive, corrective, and emergency.**

Preventive maintenance is scheduled work you do to keep things running. HVAC servicing, gutter cleaning, water heater flushing, roof inspections. This is the stuff most landlords skip because it costs money upfront. **Don't skip it.** Preventive maintenance is always cheaper than emergency repairs.

Corrective maintenance is fixing things that break. Leaky faucets, broken appliances, minor repairs. This is normal wear and tear. Budget for it.

Emergency maintenance is the middle-of-the-night stuff. Burst pipes, no heat in winter, no AC in summer, major leaks. You need to respond fast, and it's going to be expensive. This is why you have reserves.

A good rule of thumb: budget 1% of the property value per year for maintenance. If you own a $300,000 property, set aside $3,000 a year. Some years you'll spend less. Some years you'll spend more. Over time it evens out.

Cash Reserves and Discipline

This is the single most important thing that separates success-ful landlords from failed ones: reserves.

You will have vacancies. You will have expensive repairs. You will have months where the property loses money. If you don't have cash set aside to cover these situations, you're one bad month away from financial trouble.

How much should you have in reserves? A conservative rule is 6 months of debt service plus operating expenses for each property. If your mortgage and expenses total $2,000 a month, you should have $12,000 in reserves.

That sounds like a lot, and it is. But it's the difference between weathering a tough stretch and being forced to sell in a down market.

Build reserves slowly if you have to. Even $500 a month adds up. And once you have them, don't touch them unless it's a real emergency. Reserves are not for vacations or new cars. They're insurance.

Property Management: DIY or Hire?

Most investors start by managing their own properties. This makes sense when you only have one or two. You save 8 to 10% of gross rent, you learn the business, and you stay close to the operation.

But self-management has limits. It's time-consuming. It ties you to a location. It doesn't scale well. And if you're not good at it, it's stressful.

At some point, it makes sense to hire a property manager. When?

When you own enough properties that the time commitment is interfering with your job or your life.

When you live far from the properties and can't respond quickly to issues.

When you want to scale and self-management is holding you back.

Good property managers are worth every penny. Bad property managers will cost you more than they save. Interview multiple companies. Ask for references. Check online reviews. Make sure they specialize in properties like yours.

And remember: hiring a property manager doesn't mean you're hands-off. You still need to review monthly statements, approve major expenses, and make sure they're maintaining your standards. You're delegating execution, not responsibility.

Case Study: The Cost of Poor Management

Property management can make or break your investment returns. Here's what happens when it goes wrong, and what proper management looks like.

David bought a triplex in 2018 for $285,000. He decided to self-manage to save the 9% management fee. He had a full-time job and figured he could handle tenant calls in the evenings and weekends.

The first year went fine. All three units were occupied, tenants paid on time, and there were only minor maintenance issues. David handled everything himself and was proud of saving $2,500 in management fees.

Year two, things started falling apart. One tenant gave notice and moved out. David delayed listing the unit because he was busy at work. The unit sat vacant for two months before he found time to paint, clean, and market it. Lost rent: $2,000.

A second tenant started paying late consistently. David felt uncomfortable confronting them, so he let it slide. By month four, they owed $3,200 in back rent. He eventually filed for eviction, which cost $800 in legal fees and took another month. Total loss: $4,800 including legal costs and turnover.

The third tenant had a maintenance emergency on a Saturday night. David didn't have a handyman on call. He tried to fix it himself on Sunday and made it worse. He had to call an emergency plumber Monday morning. Cost: $1,200, when a proper emergency response would have cost $350.

By the end of year two, David had "saved" $2,500 in management fees but lost $8,000 to poor management decisions. The stress had affected his work performance, his wife was frustrated with the constant weekend emergencies, and he was ready to sell.

Instead, he hired a property manager for year three. The manager charged 9% of gross rents, about $2,700 per year. Here's what changed:

When a tenant moved out, the unit was cleaned, repainted, photographed, and listed within 48 hours. Average vacancy time: 12 days instead of 60 days.

When a tenant paid late, the manager sent a 3-day pay or quit notice immediately. Late payment fees were collected. Tenants learned to pay on time. No evictions needed.

When maintenance issues arose, the manager had a network

of reliable contractors with pre-negotiated rates. Emergency response time: under 2 hours. Costs: 30% lower than David had been paying.

Annual rent increases were implemented systematically. Tenants accepted them because they were market rate and professionally communicated. Annual rent growth: $120 per unit.

David's net operating income increased by $6,500 in year three compared to year two, even after paying management fees. The property ran smoothly, his stress disappeared, and he bought two more properties because he knew he could manage them professionally without consuming his life.

The lesson: the cheapest option isn't always the best option. Sometimes paying for professional management is the smartest financial decision you can make.

Building Systems That Scale

If you're managing properties yourself, even temporarily, you need systems. Without systems, you're reinventing the process every time something happens. With systems, you have checklists and procedures that ensure consistency and efficiency.

Here are the essential systems every self-managing investor needs:

Tenant screening system: Create a checklist with minimum

requirements. Credit score above 600. Income at least 3x monthly rent. No evictions in the past 7 years. Positive references from previous landlords. Employment verification.

Run the same checks on every applicant. Use the same application form. Evaluate everyone by the same criteria. This protects you legally and ensures you're selecting quality tenants consistently.

Don't shortcut screening because you're desperate to fill a vacancy. Bad tenants cost more than vacancy. Every time.

Rent collection system: Set up automatic payments through a property management platform like Cozy, Avail, or RentRedi. Tenants can pay by ACH, credit card, or debit card. Payments are automated and tracked.

Implement a late fee policy and enforce it consistently. If rent is due on the 1st with a grace period until the 5th, charge a late fee on the 6th. No exceptions. Tenants learn your boundaries by how you enforce them.

If a tenant is late twice in a row, have a conversation. If they're late a third time, start eviction proceedings. Don't let it get to four or five months of non-payment. The longer you wait, the more you lose.

Maintenance response system: Create a tiered response system. Emergency issues (no heat in winter, major water leaks, security concerns) get same-day response. Urgent issues (non-functioning appliances, minor leaks) get 24- to 48-

hour response. Non-urgent issues (cosmetic repairs, minor inconveniences) get 5- to 7-day response.

Communicate these response times to tenants so they know what to expect. Then hit your deadlines consistently. Tenants appreciate knowing their issues will be handled, even if it's not immediate.

Build a contractor database with at least two options for each service: plumbing, electrical, HVAC, handyman, appliance repair, locksmith. Get quotes from both when issues arise. This ensures competitive pricing and backup options if your primary contractor is unavailable.

Inspection system: Schedule routine inspections every 6 to 12 months. Walk the property, check for unreported damage, verify smoke detectors work, ensure tenants are maintaining the unit reasonably. Document everything with photos.

These inspections help you catch small problems before they become big ones. They also remind tenants that you're paying attention. Properties with regular inspections tend to be better maintained.

Turnover system: When a tenant gives notice, immediately create a checklist. Schedule move-out inspection. Line up cleaning crew. Get painter quotes. Order appliances if needed. List the unit while work is being done.

The goal is to minimize vacancy. Every day a unit sits empty costs you money. Investors who have this system in place turn units in 10 to 15 days. Investors without it often take 30 to 60 days or more.

Record-keeping system: Use accounting software like Stessa, Quickbooks, or even a detailed spreadsheet. Record every dollar in and out. Save receipts. Track expenses by category (mortgage, taxes, insurance, repairs, maintenance, utilities, management).

This makes tax time infinitely easier. It also gives you clear data on your property's performance. You'll know exactly where your money is going and where you might be overspending.

Review your numbers monthly. Don't wait until year-end to discover you've been losing money. Monthly reviews let you spot problems quickly and make adjustments.

These systems take time to set up initially, but they save hours every month once they're running. More importantly, they ensure nothing falls through the cracks.

The Economics of Property Management Fees

Many investors resist hiring property managers because of the cost. Let's examine whether this math makes sense.

A typical property manager charges 8 to 10% of gross collected rents, plus a leasing fee (often one month's rent) when placing new tenants. For a property generating $1,500 per month in rent, that's $135 to $150 per month in management fees, or

$1,620 to $1,800 annually.

Seems expensive. But what are you getting, and what's your time worth?

Time savings: Self-managing a property takes 5 to 10 hours per month on average. Handling tenant calls, coordinating maintenance, showing units, processing applications, collecting rent. At a conservative $50 per hour, that's $250 to $500 per month in opportunity cost. For many professionals, it's more.

If you're spending 10 hours per month to save $150, you're valuing your time at $15 per hour. Does that make sense given what you earn at your day job?

Vacancy reduction: Professional managers typically fill vacancies faster because they have systems, marketing platforms, and experience. If they reduce your average vacancy from 30 days to 15 days per turnover, they've saved you $750 in lost rent on a $1,500 per month unit.

That one benefit often pays for six months of management fees.

Better tenant quality: Professional managers screen tenants systematically. They check credit, verify income, contact references, and run background checks. They're less likely to skip steps or make exceptions.

Better tenants mean fewer late payments, fewer maintenance calls, less property damage, and longer tenancies. Hard to quantify precisely, but the impact is significant.

Maintenance cost control: Good property managers have negotiated rates with contractors. They get better prices than individual landlords calling around. They also catch maintenance issues earlier through regular inspections, preventing small problems from becoming expensive repairs.

Even a 10 to 15% reduction in maintenance costs can offset a substantial portion of management fees.

Legal compliance: Property managers understand fair housing laws, security deposit regulations, eviction procedures, and lease requirements. They keep your business compliant, reducing your risk of expensive lawsuits.

One fair housing violation or botched eviction can cost tens of thousands in legal fees and settlements. Professional management is insurance against these risks.

Scalability: If you want to own more than two or three properties, professional management becomes essential. You can't self-manage ten properties while working full-time. Professional management removes that limitation.

When you run the math honestly, property management fees often pay for themselves. You're not spending $1,800 per year. You're investing $1,800 to protect a $250,000 asset, save time, reduce risk, and enable growth.

That said, not all property managers are created equal. Some are excellent. Some are mediocre. Some are terrible. Your job is to find the excellent ones.

How to Evaluate Property Managers

If you decide to hire a property manager, don't just pick the first name that comes up on Google. Interview at least three companies. Ask detailed questions. Check references.

Here's what to ask:

How many properties do you manage, and what types? You want a manager who specializes in properties like yours. If you own small multifamily, find a manager who focuses on that segment. If you own single-family homes, find someone with SFR experience.

What's your average vacancy time? Good managers should fill vacancies in 15 to 21 days on average. If they're consistently taking 30 to 45 days, they're either overpriced, bad at marketing, or working in a difficult market.

How do you screen tenants? They should have a clear, consistent process. Minimum credit score. Income verification. Previous landlord references. Background checks. If they say they go by "feel" or "instinct," move on.

What's your maintenance response time? For emergencies, same day. For urgent issues, 24 to 48 hours. For routine issues, 3 to 5 business days. If they can't commit to these timelines, they're understaffed or disorganized.

Who are your go-to contractors, and how did you select them? They should have established relationships with licensed, insured contractors. Ask for the contractor names and verify their licenses and insurance independently.

How do you handle late rent and evictions? They should have a clear policy. Three-day notice after the grace period. Eviction filing if payment isn't received. No exceptions for sob stories. Consistency protects you.

How often will I receive financial reports, and what's included? Monthly statements are standard. They should include income, expenses, account balances, and year-to-date summaries. If they don't provide clear reporting, you won't know how your property is performing.

What are your fees, and what's not included? Management fee, leasing fee, renewal fee, inspection fee. Get everything in writing. Watch for managers who charge extra for every small service. The fee structure should be transparent and straightforward.

Can I see references from current clients? Talk to at least two or three current clients. Ask about responsiveness, communication, maintenance quality, and any problems they've encountered. If the manager won't provide references, that's a red flag.

What happens if I'm not satisfied? Understand the contract terms. Most management agreements allow either party to terminate with 30 to 60 days' notice. Be wary of contracts that lock you in for a year or more without an out clause.

The best property managers are proactive communicators. They send monthly reports without being asked. They flag issues before they become expensive. They treat your property like it's their own. When you find someone like this, hold onto them.

<h1 style="text-align:center">10</h1>

Chapter 10: Common Mistakes and Red Flags

Most real estate investors make the same mistakes. If you know what to watch for, you can avoid them.

Contractor Problems

Contractors are essential, and most are honest, skilled professionals. But some will take your money, do bad work, or disappear halfway through the job. Here's how to protect yourself:

Get multiple bids: Never hire the first contractor you talk to. Get at least three bids for any major project. This gives you a sense of market rates and lets you compare approaches.

Check references and licenses: Ask for references from recent jobs. Call them. Drive by the properties if you can. Make sure the contractor is licensed and insured.

Pay in stages, not upfront: Never pay the full amount before the work is done. Structure payments around milestones: 10% upfront, 40% at rough-in, 40% at substantial completion, 10% after final walkthrough.

Put everything in writing: Have a detailed contract that specifies scope of work, timeline, payment terms, and who's responsible for permits. Verbal agreements lead to disputes.

Watch for red flags: If a contractor asks for a huge deposit, won't put things in writing, or pushes you to start before you're ready, walk away.

Even with all these precautions, things will go wrong. Projects will run over budget. Contractors will miss deadlines. Inspectors will find issues. This is normal. Build buffer into your budget and timeline.

Loose Numbers

Most bad deals happen because someone convinced themselves the numbers worked when they didn't.

You rounded rent up by $100 a month. You assumed 95% occupancy when the market average is 85%. You underestimated repairs. You forgot to include property management fees. You assumed rents would increase 5% a year.

Death by a thousand optimistic assumptions.

The fix is brutal honesty. Use actual rent comps, not best-case scenarios. Use conservative occupancy rates. Overestimate expenses. Don't assume rents will grow unless you have data to support it.

If the deal only works under perfect conditions, it's not a good deal.

Bad Bookkeeping

You need to track income and expenses for every property. Not because it's fun, but because it's essential.

Good bookkeeping lets you see which properties are performing and which aren't. It makes tax time easier. It helps you spot problems early. And if you ever want to refinance or sell, lenders and buyers will ask for financial records.

Use software. QuickBooks, Stessa, Baselane, whatever. Don't use spreadsheets. Don't keep receipts in a shoebox. Set up a separate bank account for each property or at least for your rental business as a whole.

Track everything: rent collected, expenses paid, maintenance costs, vacancy days, late fees. Review your numbers monthly. This doesn't take long, and it's the difference between running a business and running a mess.

Emotional Buying

Real estate is tangible. You can walk through it. You can see the neighborhood. This makes it easy to get emotionally attached, which is fine if you're buying a home to live in. It's dangerous if you're buying an investment.

The fix is discipline. Go back to your buy box. Go back to your numbers. If it doesn't fit, walk away. There's always another deal.

Buy with your calculator, not your heart.

Scaling Too Early

After you buy your first property, something shifts. You start thinking bigger. You want to buy five more. You want to quit your job and do this full-time.

Slow down.

Real estate rewards patience. Your first property teaches you how to underwrite deals, manage tenants, and handle maintenance. Your second property teaches you how to scale systems. Your third property shows you whether you actually like this business.

Don't quit your job until you have enough cash flow to replace your income and enough reserves to handle problems. Don't leverage yourself to the max to buy more properties. Don't assume everything will keep working just because it worked once.

Scale deliberately. Prove the model with one or two properties. Then grow.

Ignoring Red Flags

When you're evaluating a property, sometimes you'll see something that doesn't feel right. Maybe the seller is evasive about financials. Maybe the property has deferred maintenance everywhere you look.

When you see red flags, don't rationalize them away. If the seller won't provide rent rolls, walk away. If the property needs $50,000 in repairs and you only budgeted $20,000, walk away. If your gut says something's wrong, listen to it.

You will miss out on deals. That's fine. It's better to miss a good deal than to close a bad one.

Case Study: When Red Flags Get Ignored

Real estate education often focuses on what to do right. Let's look at what happens when investors ignore obvious warning signs.

Tom found what looked like an incredible deal in 2019. A fourplex listed at $320,000 in a neighborhood where similar properties sold for $400,000. The seller claimed the units each rented for $950 per month, which would have been excellent cash flow.

Tom's first red flag appeared during the showing. Three of the four units had tenants who weren't available for viewing. The seller said they worked odd hours. The fourth unit was empty and needed significant work.

Red flag number two: the seller couldn't produce rent rolls or lease agreements. He said his "system" was informal and he'd get the information later. Tom should have walked away. Instead, he rationalized. He thought, "I'll just verify everything during due diligence."

Red flag number three: the property inspection revealed $35,000 in deferred maintenance. Old roof, failing HVAC systems, outdated electrical, plumbing issues. Tom should have either walked away or negotiated a price reduction equal to the repair costs. Instead, he negotiated a $15,000 credit and convinced himself he could handle the rest.

Red flag number four: during escrow, Tom tried to contact the existing tenants to verify rents. Two never responded. One said she'd been paying $750, not $950. Tom was running out of time before his financing commitment expired. He closed anyway.

After closing, reality hit. The two non-responsive tenants didn't exist. The units were vacant and in worse condition than he'd thought. The one legitimate tenant was indeed paying

$750 and had no intention of accepting a rent increase. Getting the vacant units rent-ready cost $45,000, not $35,000, because the inspection missed issues that only became apparent during renovation.

By the time Tom had all four units rented at realistic rates of $800 per month, he'd spent $68,000 in unexpected costs and lost $12,000 in rental income during the six-month renovation. His $320,000 "deal" had actually cost him $400,000 all-in, and it barely cash flowed.

Every red flag he ignored came back to cost him money. He could have walked away at multiple points. He didn't, because he wanted the deal to work. The lesson: when multiple red flags appear, the universe is trying to tell you something. Listen.

The Financial Mistakes That Kill Investors

Beyond operational issues, many investors fail because of fundamental financial mistakes. These are the ones that end careers.

Mistake: No reserves. Starting real estate investing without cash reserves is like skydiving without a backup parachute. Eventually, something will go wrong.

Rebecca bought her first rental property with every dollar she had saved. Down payment, closing costs, and minor repairs exhausted her savings. The property cash flowed $200 per month, which she thought was sufficient.

Four months after closing, the HVAC system failed. Replacement cost: $6,500. Rebecca didn't have the money. She put it on a credit card at 18% interest. Two months later, a tenant moved out unexpectedly. Unit renovation and two months of vacancy: $4,000 more on the credit card.

Within six months, Rebecca had $10,500 in high-interest credit card debt. The monthly minimum payments ate up her entire cash flow plus some of her W-2 income. She was in a hole, and the property that was supposed to build wealth was costing her money every month.

Eventually, she sold the property to pay off the debt. After transaction costs, she broke even. Two years of stress for zero return.

The solution: maintain reserves equal to six months of expenses per property, minimum. Better yet, keep reserves equal to one year. This covers vacancies, repairs, and unexpected emergencies. Yes, it means buying properties more slowly. That's the price of safety.

Mistake: Over-leveraging. Using maximum leverage to buy as many properties as possible creates massive risk when markets soften or when multiple properties have issues simultaneously.

Carlos bought five properties in 18 months, all with 10% down using aggressive financing. His cash flow across all five properties was $800 per month combined. Thin, but he rationalized that appreciation and rent growth would improve the numbers.

Then 2023 happened. Insurance premiums increased 40% across all five properties. Property taxes increased 8%. Interest rates on his adjustable-rate mortgages adjusted upward. His $800 monthly cash flow became a $300 monthly loss.

Carlos couldn't afford to subsidize five properties indefinitely. He tried to sell two, but the market had softened. He eventually sold three at a loss just to reduce his monthly bleeding. His aggressive leverage, which looked smart during the good times, destroyed him when conditions changed.

The solution: use conservative leverage. 20 to 25% down payment. Fixed-rate financing. Build cash flow cushion that can absorb expense increases. Accept that you'll buy fewer properties, but the ones you buy will be sustainable.

Mistake: Counting on appreciation. Buying properties that only make sense if they appreciate is speculation, not investing.

Linda bought a condo in a hot market for $450,000 in 2021. After expenses and HOA fees, the property had negative cash flow of $300 per month. She accepted this because everyone said the market was going up 10 to 15% per year.

By 2024, the market had softened. Her condo was worth $420,000. She'd subsidized it for three years at $300 per month, losing $10,800 in cash flow. Plus she'd lost $30,000 in value. Total loss: $40,800.

If she sold, she'd lose money after transaction costs. If she held, she'd keep bleeding cash. There was no good option.

The solution: only buy properties that cash flow from day one. Appreciation is a bonus, not a requirement. If your deal depends on appreciation to work, it's not a deal.

Mistake: Ignoring taxes. Real estate generates taxable income. If you don't plan for it, April can be a very unpleasant surprise.

Marcus owned four rental properties generating $24,000 per year in cash flow after all expenses and debt service. He thought that was his profit. He didn't account for the tax burden.

Rental income is taxed as ordinary income. Marcus was in the 24% federal bracket plus 5% state. Even after depreciation deductions, he owed about $4,500 in additional taxes. He hadn't set any money aside for this because he didn't understand rental income taxation.

He scrambled to pay the taxes, which wiped out five months of his cash flow. The next year, he worked with a CPA to plan properly. But the first year was painful.

The solution: work with a real estate CPA before you buy your first property. Understand your tax situation. Set aside 20 to 30% of your cash flow for taxes until you know exactly what your liability will be. Better to over-save and get a refund than to under-save and owe money you don't have.

The Hidden Costs Beginners Miss

Beyond the obvious mistakes, there are hidden costs that trip up new investors. Here are the ones nobody talks about:

Utility turnover costs: When a tenant moves out, you're responsible for utilities until the next tenant moves in. For a month of vacancy, that could be $150 to $300. Budget for this.

Cleaning and carpet replacement: Even with a cleaning deposit, you'll often need to hire professional cleaners and replace carpet. Budget $500 to $1,000 per turnover.

Lock changes: You should change locks between every tenant for security. Budget $100 to $200 per turnover.

HOA fees during vacancy: If the property has HOA fees, you're paying them whether it's occupied or not. Factor this into vacancy calculations.

Marketing costs: Photos, listing fees, background check services. Budget $200 to $300 per turnover.

Your time: Showings, phone calls, application processing. Even if you don't pay yourself, there's an opportunity cost.

Most beginners budget only for the mortgage during vacancy. They forget about these other costs. When reality hits, their thin cash flow disappears.

Build these costs into your analysis before you buy. If a property can't absorb realistic turnover costs, it's not a good deal.

Learning From Failed Deals

One of the best things you can do as an investor is analyze the deals that didn't work out. Not just the ones you passed on, but the ones that other investors bought and struggled with.

Join local investor groups and pay attention when people share their mistakes. Someone bought a property with foundation issues they didn't catch in inspection. Someone got stuck with a tenant who stopped paying and took eight months to evict. Someone underestimated rehab costs by $30,000.

These stories are valuable. Take notes. Ask questions. Learn from other people's mistakes so you don't have to make them yourself.

Create a "lessons learned" document. Every time you hear about a mistake, write it down along with how to avoid it. Review this document before analyzing deals. It's like having a checklist of red flags.

The investors who progress fastest are the ones who learn from other people's expensive mistakes, not just their own.

The Warning Signs of Bad Tenants

Tenant problems cause more stress and cost more money than most other real estate issues. Learning to spot problem tenants before they become your problem saves enormous headaches.

Warning sign: They push to skip the application process. Good tenants understand that screening is normal. They provide documents promptly. They answer questions clearly. Problem tenants make excuses, ask if you "really need" to check references, or try to charm their way past the process.

If someone resists screening, decline the application. No exceptions.

Warning sign: They have a great excuse for everything. Bad credit? It was their ex's fault. Previous eviction? The landlord was unreasonable. Can't verify income? They're paid in cash. Lost their job? It's temporary and they have savings.

Maybe these explanations are legitimate. But when someone has multiple explanations for multiple problems, you're likely looking at a pattern of dysfunction. Pass.

Warning sign: They're in a desperate rush to move in. Legitimate tenants have notice periods. They plan moves in advance. Tenants who need to move in immediately are often running from something: an eviction in process, a situation with a previous landlord, or legal problems.

Desperate tenants make bad decisions. You don't want to be their bad decision.

Warning sign: They want to pay several months in advance. This sounds great, but it's often a red flag. Tenants offering large upfront payments may be trying to avoid credit checks or compensate for known problems. They might also be using the property for illegal activities and want to secure it quickly.

Accept one month's rent plus security deposit. No more, no less.

Warning sign: They ask unusual questions. Can they repaint? Can they install security systems? Can they change the locks? Do you do regular inspections? How often do you visit the property?

These questions suggest they plan to do things you won't approve of. Or they don't want you visiting the property. Either way, it's concerning.

Warning sign: Their story keeps changing. They said they work in healthcare, then you hear them mention restaurant work. They said they have one dog, then mention their two cats. They said their credit score is 680, but the report shows 590.

People who lie about small things will lie about big things. And tenants who lie before they move in will lie while they're your tenants.

The best way to avoid bad tenants is to have clear screening criteria and enforce them consistently. No exceptions for anyone, no matter how charming or sympathetic. Your criteria exist to protect you. Trust them.

How to Recover From Mistakes

Despite your best efforts, you'll make mistakes. Properties will underperform. Tenants will cause problems. Renovations will go over budget. Markets will soften at the wrong time.

The question isn't if you'll make mistakes. It's how you'll respond when you do.

First response: stop the bleeding. When something goes wrong, your first priority is preventing it from getting worse. Tenant not paying? Start eviction immediately. Property losing money every month? Figure out why and fix it or sell. Contractor doing poor work? Fire them and find someone better.

Don't wait. Don't hope it improves on its own. Act decisively to contain the damage.

Second response: analyze what happened. After you've stopped the bleeding, figure out why it happened. Did you ignore red flags? Did you skip due diligence? Did you make optimistic assumptions that didn't pan out? Did you fail to maintain proper reserves?

Be brutally honest. Don't blame external factors exclusively. Even if bad luck played a role, there's usually something you could have done differently.

Third response: implement systems to prevent recurrence. If you bought a property without proper reserves and got burned, commit to never buying without six months of reserves again. If you hired a bad tenant because you skipped reference checks, commit to thorough screening forever.

Learn the lesson once. Don't repeat the same mistakes.

Fourth response: move forward. Don't let one bad experience paralyze you. Real estate investing involves risk. Some deals will go wrong. That doesn't mean the strategy is flawed. It means you're human.

Process the mistake, extract the lesson, adjust your approach, and keep going. The investors who quit after their first mistake never build wealth. The investors who persist, despite mistakes, eventually succeed.

Many successful investors have war stories about terrible deals early in their careers. They bought properties they shouldn't have. They hired awful tenants. They over-leveraged at the wrong time. But they learned, adjusted, and continued. That's why they're successful now.

Your mistakes don't define you. Your response to them does.

11

Chapter 11: Growing a Portfolio Intentionally

Scaling a real estate portfolio is not about buying as many properties as possible as fast as possible. It's about building a foundation that supports growth without breaking.

Most investors who scale too quickly either burn out or go broke. The ones who scale successfully do it deliberately, with systems, capital, and a clear plan.

Refinance Strategies

Refinancing is one of the most powerful tools for scaling. It lets you pull equity out of properties you already own and redeploy that capital into new deals.

Here's how it works: You buy a property for $300,000. You put 25% down and finance the rest. Five years later, the property is worth $400,000 and you've paid down some principal. You refinance, pulling out cash while keeping the property.

You can use that cash to buy another property. Your original property still generates income, but now you've recycled your capital into a second deal.

This is the BRRRR strategy: Buy, Rehab, Rent, Refinance, Repeat. It works, but it requires discipline. You need to make sure the property still cash flows after you refinance. If the new mortgage payment eats all your cash flow, you've just added risk without adding income.

Be conservative with refinancing. Don't pull out so much equity that the property becomes a financial liability. And remember, refinancing comes with costs: appraisal fees, closing costs, and potentially a higher interest rate if you refinance into a DSCR or portfolio loan.

Partnerships: What Breaks Them

At some point, you might consider partnering with someone to buy properties. Maybe they have capital and you have expertise. Maybe you both bring different skills to the table.

Partnerships can work, but they're fragile. Most partnerships break because of one of three things:

Unequal effort: One partner does all the work while the other collects checks. Resentment builds. Eventually someone walks.

Poor communication: Decisions get made without agreement. Money gets spent without discussion. Small frustrations compound.

Misaligned goals: One partner wants to hold forever. The other wants to sell and cash out. One wants to scale aggressively. The other wants to stay conservative.

If you're going to partner, put everything in writing. Who's responsible for what? How are decisions made? How is profit split? What happens if someone wants to exit?

Have those conversations before you buy the property, not after things go wrong.

Deal Flow vs. Deal Quality

As you grow, you'll feel pressure to keep buying. You'll meet other investors who brag about how many properties they own. You'll worry that you're falling behind.

Ignore that.

Deal flow is not the same as deal quality. Buying 10 mediocre properties is worse than buying 3 great ones. More properties mean more management, more risk, and more capital tied up. If those properties don't generate strong returns, you're just busy, not successful.

Stay disciplined. Stick to your buy box. Wait for good deals. It's better to buy one property a year that cash flows well than to buy five properties a year that barely break even.

Avoiding Over-Leverage

Leverage is a tool. It lets you control more assets with less capital. But it's also dangerous if you misuse it.

Over-leverage looks like this: You own five properties, each with 90% financing. Your cash flow is thin. You have minimal reserves. One vacancy or major repair and you can't cover the mortgages. You're forced to sell in a bad market or worse, you lose properties to foreclosure.

The solution is simple: maintain equity. As your properties appreciate, don't immediately refinance and pull out all the equity. Leave some buffer. Aim for at least 20 to 30% equity in each property.

And keep building reserves. The more properties you own, the more cash you need on hand to weather problems.

When to Sell

Most real estate advice focuses on buying and holding forever. "Never sell. Build generational wealth."

That's great advice until it's not.

Sometimes selling makes sense. Maybe the property has appreciated significantly and you'd rather lock in gains than hold and hope for more. Maybe the neighborhood is declining and cash flow is getting harder. Maybe you want to exit a market and redeploy capital elsewhere.

Selling doesn't mean you failed. It means you're managing a portfolio, not collecting trophies.

Here's when selling makes sense:

When the property has appreciated to the point where the cap rate no longer justifies holding it.

When management is getting harder and the stress outweighs the return.

When you can redeploy the capital into better opportunities.

When you no longer want exposure to that market or property type.

1031 exchanges let you defer capital gains if you reinvest the proceeds into another property. That's useful if you want to stay in real estate. But don't feel obligated to. Sometimes it makes more sense to take the tax hit, simplify your life, and move on.

The Long Game

Growing a portfolio takes years, not months. You'll have years where you buy multiple properties. You'll have years where you don't buy anything. You'll have years where you sell properties that no longer fit your strategy.

That's all normal. The goal isn't to hit some arbitrary number of properties. The goal is to build a portfolio that generates income, appreciates over time, and supports your financial goals.

Stay patient. Stay disciplined. Keep your costs low, your reserves high, and your leverage moderate. Do that for 10 or 15 years, and you'll build something meaningful.

Case Study: Three Different Scaling Paths

Portfolio growth isn't one-size-fits-all. Here are three investors who scaled differently, each achieving their goals through approaches that matched their circumstances and temperaments.

Path One: The Slow and Steady Accumulator

Jennifer's goal was to replace her $75,000 annual salary by age 50. She was 32 when she bought her first property, giving her 18 years to build her portfolio.

She bought one property per year for the first eight years. Each property was a duplex or triplex in stable neighborhoods. She put 25% down on every property, financed with 30-year fixed mortgages, and each property cash flowed $300 to $500 per month after all expenses.

Years 1 through 4: One property per year. Total portfolio: 4 properties, generating combined cash flow of $1,600 per month.

Years 5 through 8: One property per year. Total portfolio: 8 properties, generating $3,200 per month combined. She used cash flow from existing properties plus W-2 savings for down payments.

Years 9 through 12: She paused acquisitions and focused on paying down mortgages on her first four properties. She directed all rental cash flow toward principal payments on these properties while maintaining reserves.

Years 13 through 15: Three of her first four properties were paid off. Cash flow from these properties: $4,500 per month. She used this to accelerate mortgage paydown on properties 5 through 8.

Years 16 through 18: She bought two more properties using cash flow and refinancing equity from paid-off properties. By year 18, she owned 10 properties. Six were paid off, four had mortgages. Combined cash flow: $7,200 per month, exceeding her target.

Jennifer's approach required patience. She never felt like she was getting rich quickly. But compounding did its work. After 18 years, she had a portfolio generating more income than her job, mostly from paid-off properties that required minimal management.

Path Two: The BRRRR Recycler

Marcus wanted to scale faster. He had access to capital through a home equity line of credit and planned to use the BRRRR method: Buy, Rehab, Rent, Refinance, Repeat.

Year 1: He bought a distressed triplex for $185,000, spent $40,000 on rehab, and refinanced at $280,000 after the work was complete. He pulled out his initial $225,000 investment, and the property cash flowed $450 per month with the new, higher mortgage.

Year 2: He bought two more properties using the same method. Each deal required 6 to 8 months from purchase to refinance. By year-end, he owned three properties, all with minimal capital remaining in them, generating combined cash flow of $1,200 per month.

Years 3 through 5: He continued at a pace of two to three properties per year. By year 5, he owned 11 properties. His combined cash flow was $4,800 per month, but he carried higher debt levels than Jennifer because each property was refinanced at 75 to 80% LTV after rehab.

Years 6 through 8: Marcus paused acquisitions. The pace had been exhausting, and he needed to consolidate. He focused on stabilizing operations, improving property management systems, and building reserves. Some properties appreciated, allowing him to refinance again and access equity without taking on additional properties.

Year 9 and beyond: Marcus resumed buying, but more selectively. He'd learned that rapid scaling created operational challenges. He slowed to one to two properties per year, focusing on quality over quantity.

By year 10, Marcus owned 15 properties. His cash flow was higher than Jennifer's at the same point, but his stress level had also been higher. He'd experienced contractor problems, refinancing delays, and operational chaos during the fast-growth years. But he'd achieved scale faster than the slow-and-steady approach would have allowed.

Path Three: The Market Switcher

Sophie started in expensive markets and shifted to affordable ones as her strategy evolved.

Years 1 through 3: She bought three single-family homes in her local market, a suburban California area with high prices and low cash flow. Each property was purchased at $550,000 to $650,000 with 20% down. Combined cash flow was minimal, about $600 per month total, but properties appreciated strongly. Over three years, her properties increased in value by a combined $300,000.

Year 4: Sophie realized she couldn't scale in her local market. Prices were too high, and cash flow was too low. She sold one property, netting $180,000 in proceeds after paying off the mortgage and transaction costs. She used this to buy three duplexes in a Midwest market where properties were $180,000 to $220,000 each. These properties generated $400 to $500 per month in cash flow each.

Years 5 through 7: She continued the strategy: holding two properties in California for appreciation, buying cash-flowing properties in affordable markets with the equity she extracted. She used 1031 exchanges when possible to defer taxes.

By year 7, she owned 2 properties in California and 8 properties in affordable markets. The California properties had appreciated substantially but generated little cash flow. The out-of-state properties generated $3,600 per month in combined cash flow and provided stable income.

Sophie's approach combined appreciation and cash flow. She used high-appreciation markets to build equity, then redeployed that equity into cash-flowing markets. It required more complexity managing properties in multiple states, but it allowed her to scale while maintaining strong cash flow.

Three investors. Three strategies. All three built successful portfolios. The right strategy isn't universal. It depends on your market, your capital, your goals, and your tolerance for complexity.

The Mathematics of Sustainable Growth

Many investors scale too fast and collapse. Others scale too slowly and miss opportunities. The key is understanding the mathematics of sustainable growth.

Capital recycling speed: How quickly can you redeploy capital into new deals? If you're using the BRRRR method, you can recycle capital every 6 to 12 months. If you're buying and holding with traditional financing, your capital is locked up until you sell or refinance years later.

Marcus recycled capital quickly, allowing him to scale faster. Jennifer's capital was locked up, forcing slower growth. Both approaches work. You need to understand which one you're using and plan accordingly.

Cash flow allocation: What percentage of your cash flow should you reinvest in new deals versus hold as reserves? Conservative investors might hold 50% of cash flow in reserves and only deploy 50% toward new purchases. Aggressive investors might reinvest 80% and hold only 20% in reserves.

There's no right answer, but understand the trade-offs. Higher reserves mean slower growth but more stability. Lower reserves mean faster growth but more risk.

Jennifer held high reserves and grew slowly. Marcus held lower reserves and grew faster but experienced stress when multiple properties had issues simultaneously. Know your risk tolerance and plan accordingly.

Leverage limits: How much debt can you safely carry? This depends on your income, your cash flow, and your reserves.

A common rule of thumb: your total debt service across all properties should not exceed 50% of your gross rental income.

If your properties generate $10,000 per month in rent, your combined mortgage payments shouldn't exceed $5,000. This ensures you have margin for expenses, vacancies, and unexpected issues.

Marcus pushed leverage higher and got away with it because his properties cash flowed well. But when expenses increased, his thin margins created problems. Jennifer used lower leverage and slept better at night.

Time investment: How much time do you have to dedicate to real estate? Marcus scaled fast but spent 20 to 30 hours per week managing rehabs, coordinating contractors, and handling tenant issues. Jennifer scaled slowly and spent 5 to 10 hours per week because her properties required less intensive management.

If you have a demanding full-time job, scaling like Marcus is probably unrealistic. If you're working part-time or have flexible hours, you can handle more complexity.

The math of sustainable growth boils down to this: grow as fast as your capital, cash flow, systems, and time allow, but don't exceed your capacity in any of these areas. When you push past your limits, mistakes happen and the whole operation becomes stressful and fragile.

When to Pause, When to Sell, When to Refinance

Portfolio management isn't just about buying more properties. It's about knowing when to pause, when to exit, and when to reposition.

When to pause acquisitions:

You're stretched thin operationally. If you're constantly dealing with tenant issues, maintenance emergencies, and contractor problems, you've exceeded your management capacity. Pause buying and build better systems.

Your reserves are depleted. If unexpected expenses in your existing properties have consumed your reserves, stop buying and rebuild your cash cushion. Buying without reserves is gambling.

Your cash flow is declining. If expenses are increasing faster than rents, or if you're experiencing higher vacancy, pause and figure out what's wrong. Don't add more properties until you've stabilized what you have.

The market feels overheated. If prices are climbing fast, competition is fierce, and cash flow is becoming impossible to find, pause. Overpaying in a hot market creates problems when the market normalizes.

You need to catch your breath. Scaling is exhausting. If you're burned out, pause. It's better to take six months off and recharge than to make bad decisions because you're tired and stressed.

Pausing doesn't mean quitting. It means consolidating, stabilizing, and preparing for the next phase of growth.

When to sell properties:

The property no longer fits your strategy. Maybe you bought single-family homes initially but now focus on small multifamily. Maybe you bought in a market you no longer want exposure to. Selling and redeploying capital into properties that fit your current strategy makes sense.

The property requires too much management time relative to returns. Some properties are high-maintenance and low-return. If you have a property that constantly demands attention and barely cash flows, sell it. Redeploy that capital into something better.

You can't afford necessary capital improvements. If a property needs a $25,000 roof replacement and you don't have the capital, selling might be better than taking on debt or depleting reserves. Sometimes walking away is the smart move.

You can achieve significant gains. If a property has appreciated substantially and selling would allow you to diversify into multiple properties or a different market, consider it. Don't sell just because something went up in value, but if the proceeds would significantly improve your portfolio, it's worth considering.

When to refinance:

You've built substantial equity through appreciation or pay-down. If a property has increased in value by 20% or more since you bought it, you may be able to refinance, pull out equity, and still maintain positive cash flow. This allows you to access capital without selling.

Interest rates have dropped significantly. If rates are 1.5 to 2 percentage points lower than your current mortgage, refinancing can reduce your monthly payment and improve cash flow. Just make sure the closing costs don't negate the savings.

You want to consolidate short-term debt. If you've used credit cards or hard money loans for rehabs or repairs, refinancing to consolidate this debt into a mortgage with lower rates and longer terms makes sense.

You need capital for another opportunity. If you've found a great deal but lack down payment funds, refinancing an existing property to pull out equity can provide the capital. Just make sure the property you're refinancing still cash flows after the new, higher mortgage payment.

Portfolio management is dynamic. You're constantly evaluating what you own, what's working, and where to deploy capital next. The investors who treat real estate as buy-and-forget passive investments usually underperform. The investors who actively manage, adjust, and optimize their portfolios over time build the most wealth.

The Psychological Side of Scaling

The challenges of scaling aren't just financial and operational. They're psychological. As your portfolio grows, so does the mental burden.

More properties mean more problems. When you own one property, you might have one tenant call per month. When you own ten, you might have two or three calls per week. More vacancies. More maintenance issues. More decisions to make.

Some investors handle this easily. Others find it overwhelming. Know yourself. If you're someone who stresses about every tenant call, rapid scaling might not be right for you. If you can compartmentalize and handle problems as they arise without losing sleep, you can probably scale faster.

There's no shame in acknowledging that ten properties is your limit. Building a portfolio of ten well-managed, cash-flowing properties that you can handle comfortably is better than building twenty properties that consume your life and make you miserable.

Jennifer found that eight properties was her sweet spot. She could manage operations comfortably, the income was substantial, and she didn't feel overwhelmed. When she hit eight, she paused acquisitions and focused on optimization rather than expansion.

Marcus found he could handle fifteen properties, but only after hiring a property manager. Self-managing fifteen properties was too much. Hiring a manager made scaling sustainable.

Sophie found that managing properties across multiple states required systems and delegation. She couldn't self-manage remotely. She hired property managers in each market and accepted the 8 to 10% management fee as a cost of scaling.

Understand your psychological limits and build your portfolio accordingly. Scaling shouldn't make you miserable. If it does, you're doing it wrong.

Creating Your Investment Entity Structure

At some point, you'll need to think about how your properties are titled and what entity structure makes sense. This is where a real estate attorney and CPA become essential.

Common structures:

Individual ownership: You own the property in your personal name. Simple, but offers no liability protection. If someone sues, they can go after all your personal assets. Properly underwritten property insurance is an important tool to help keep you insulated in this phase.

LLC: Limited Liability Company. Provides liability protection. If someone sues over a property issue, they can only go after the assets in that LLC, not your personal assets. Many investors create separate LLCs for each property or group of properties.

Series LLC: Available in some states. One LLC can have multiple "series," each with its own assets and liabilities. Like having multiple LLCs under one umbrella. Simpler administration than having separate LLCs.

S Corporation or C Corporation: More complex, typically used once you have significant portfolio or rental income. Offers additional tax planning opportunities but comes with more compliance requirements.

Talk to a CPA before setting up any entity. The right structure depends on your state, your income, your goals, and your risk tolerance. What works for an investor in Texas might not work for one in California.

And remember: setting up an LLC costs money, requires annual filings, and adds complexity to financing and taxes. Don't rush into it. Many investors wait until they own 3 to 5 properties before setting up entities.

Using 1031 Exchanges Strategically

A 1031 exchange lets you defer capital gains taxes when you sell a property by reinvesting the proceeds into another property. It's a powerful tool, but it's also complex.

Here's how it works: You sell a property and have 45 days to identify potential replacement properties. You then have 180 days from the sale date to close on one or more of those identified properties.

The replacement property must be of equal or greater value,

and you must reinvest all proceeds to fully defer taxes.

When does a 1031 make sense?

You're selling one property to buy another and want to avoid paying taxes on the gain.

You're consolidating: selling multiple smaller properties to buy one larger property.

You're upgrading: selling a property in a weaker market to buy in a stronger one.

When might you skip the 1031?

You need liquidity. Maybe you want to cash out, pay the taxes, and simplify your life.

The properties you'd exchange into don't meet your criteria. Don't buy a bad deal just to avoid taxes.

You're in a low tax bracket this year. The tax hit might be manageable.

If you do a 1031, work with a qualified intermediary. They hold the proceeds and facilitate the exchange. Don't try to do this yourself. One mistake can disqualify the entire exchange.

Building Systems That Scale

The difference between owning 3 properties and owning 10 properties isn't just more properties. It's having systems that handle the increased complexity without requiring 10x more time.

Here are systems to build:

Rent collection: Use online platforms like Cozy, Avail, or TenantCloud. Tenants pay online, you get notifications, late fees are automatic. No more chasing checks.

Maintenance requests: Use a portal or email system where tenants submit requests with photos. You or your property manager can track status, assign vendors, and maintain records. This eliminates the "he said, she said" of verbal requests.

Vendor management: Build a list of reliable contractors, plumbers, electricians, and HVAC technicians. Get their rates in advance. When something breaks, you're not scrambling to find someone.

Financial tracking: Use property management software or accounting software that categorizes transactions automatically. This makes monthly reviews and tax preparation effortless.

Document storage: Keep all leases, inspections, and correspondence in a cloud-based system like Google Drive or Dropbox. You can access everything from anywhere.

Standard operating procedures: Write down how you handle common situations. How do you screen tenants? What's your move-in process? What do you do when rent is late? Having written procedures ensures consistency and makes it easy to train a property manager or assistant later.

These systems take time to set up, but they're force multipliers. They let you manage 10 properties in the same time it used to take to manage 3.

12

Chapter 12: Working With (Not Against) the Industry

Here's the truth most new investors learn the hard way: the real estate industry isn't your enemy. It's a tool. And like any tool, it works better when you understand how to use it.

A lot of new investors try to circumvent agents, avoid commissions, and go direct to sellers because they think that's how you get better deals. Sometimes it is. Often it's not.

This chapter is about understanding the industry well enough to use it to your advantage instead of fighting it at every turn.

Why New Investors Try to Circumvent Agents

It makes intuitive sense. If a property is listed at $300,000 and the seller is paying a 6% commission, that's $18,000 going to agents. If you could buy directly from the seller, maybe you could negotiate a better price or at least save some of that cost.

So new investors send direct mail, cold call, drive for dollars, and try to find off-market deals. And sometimes it works.

But here's what they don't realize: finding off-market deals takes time, money, and consistency. You're competing with wholesalers, other investors, and people who do this full-time. For every off-market deal you close, you might have made 500 calls or sent 2,000 mailers.

Meanwhile, there are deals on the MLS that make sense right now. You're just ignoring them because you're chasing the idea of off-market.

Where That Logic Does Make Sense

Going off-market makes sense in a few situations:

You're buying in volume and you've built a lead generation system that works.

You have deep relationships in a specific neighborhood and people come to you when they want to sell.

You're targeting distressed properties that wouldn't qualify for traditional financing and need a cash buyer.

If any of those apply, go for it. But if you're a new investor buying your first property, off-market probably isn't the best use of your time.

Where It Quietly Costs You Money

Here's what most people miss: agents don't just open doors and write offers. Good agents bring market knowledge, speed, and access that you don't have on your own.

A good agent knows what properties are about to hit the market. They know which listings are overpriced and which are fairly valued. They know the neighborhoods, the comps, and the trends. They can help you move faster and avoid mistakes.

When you skip the agent, you lose that. You're analyzing deals in a vacuum. You don't know if $300,000 is a good price or a terrible one. You're guessing.

And if you're wrong, it costs you more than any commission would have.

How Good Agents Increase Exit Value

Here's something most investors don't think about: the agent you use to buy the property might also help you sell it five or ten years later.

If you build a relationship with a good agent, they become a long-term resource. They can help you evaluate whether now is the right time to sell. They can market the property effectively.

They can bring you qualified buyers and help you close fast.

A good exit can make or break your return. If you sell for 5% more because your agent marketed the property well, that's real money. More than you saved by trying to avoid working with agents in the first place.

Using Agents Effectively

A good agent can help you refine your buy box based on market reality. They can set up automatic alerts so you see new listings immediately. They can access deals before they hit the MLS.

Look for agents who work with other investors. Ask for referrals. Interview multiple agents before you commit. Find someone who understands your strategy and respects your process.

The best agent relationships are long-term. You buy your first property with them. Then your second. Over time, they learn exactly what you're looking for, and they bring you deals before they even hit the market.

Case Study: The Cost of Fighting the System

Understanding how to work with the industry rather than against it becomes clear when you see what happens when investors try to do everything themselves.

Eric was determined to minimize costs on his first rental

property purchase. He refused to work with a buyer's agent to save the commission. He hired the cheapest inspector he could find. He used an online lender with the lowest advertised rate. He avoided hiring an attorney for the closing.

The property was listed at $215,000. Eric offered $205,000 directly to the listing agent. The seller accepted, and Eric thought he'd gotten a deal by avoiding representation.

What Eric didn't know: the property had foundation issues that a thorough inspector would have caught. His budget inspector missed them. Cost to repair after closing: $18,000.

What Eric also didn't know: the online lender's "lowest rate" came with higher closing costs and an inflexible approval process. When issues came up during the transaction, the lender couldn't adapt. Eric nearly lost the deal and had to scramble to find backup financing, costing him an extra $3,500 in fees.

What Eric finally learned: the absence of an attorney meant he didn't understand several clauses in the contract that favored the seller. He accepted liability for certain issues that a competent attorney would have negotiated out of the deal.

By trying to save $6,000 in commissions and fees, Eric ended up spending an extra $21,500 in problems he didn't see coming. He also missed out on market knowledge that an experienced agent would have provided, overpaid relative to comparable properties, and dealt with months of stress from the foundation repairs.

Compare this to Rachel's experience. She worked with an investor-friendly real estate agent who took 3% commission. The agent showed her fifteen properties over two months, helped her understand market pricing, connected her with a thorough inspector, recommended a local lender who specialized in investment properties, and introduced her to a real estate attorney.

The property Rachel bought was listed at $240,000. Her agent negotiated it down to $230,000 because she had comparable sales data showing it was overpriced. The inspector found $8,000 in needed repairs, which Rachel's attorney used to negotiate a $10,000 seller credit. Her lender closed on time with no issues because they specialized in investor transactions.

Rachel paid $6,900 in commission to her agent. But she saved $10,000 on the purchase price, got a $10,000 seller credit for repairs, and avoided the mistakes that cost Eric tens of thousands. Net benefit of working with professionals: significant.

The lesson: working with experienced professionals isn't a cost. It's insurance. The right agent, lender, inspector, and attorney prevent expensive mistakes and often save you more than they cost.

Building a Professional Network That Compounds

The most successful real estate investors aren't lone wolves. They're connected to networks of other investors, agents, lenders, contractors, and property managers who bring them opportunities and help them avoid problems.

Here's how to build that network deliberately:

Start with local real estate investor meetups. Every major city has at least one monthly meetup, often hosted by local real estate investment associations. Attend consistently. Show up monthly for at least six months before expecting results.

At these meetings, don't pitch yourself or your deals. Instead, ask questions and listen. Learn what others are doing, what markets they're focused on, and what challenges they're facing. Offer value when you can. If someone mentions they're looking for a contractor, share your guy if you have one. If someone asks about financing, share what you've learned.

Over time, people will remember you as someone who shows up regularly and contributes. When they have a deal they can't take, they'll think of you. When they need a partner, they'll reach out. Networks reward consistency and generosity more than any other traits.

Connect with agents who specialize in investor properties. Don't wait until you're ready to buy to start these relationships. Reach out now. Tell them you're building a portfolio and want to understand the market. Ask if you can meet quarterly to review market conditions even if you're not actively buying.

Most investor-focused agents are happy to educate serious buyers because they know it builds long-term business. Schedule quarterly coffee meetings or calls. Ask what's working in the market, what price ranges are competitive, and where opportunities might exist. When you're ready to buy, you'll already have a relationship with someone who knows your strategy.

Attend property showings even when you're not buying. If you're not ready to purchase but you've connected with an agent, ask if you can tag along to showings occasionally. This lets you see properties firsthand, learn what condition really means, understand pricing relative to quality, and build rapport with your agent. Most agents are fine with this if you're respectful of their time and serious about eventually buying.

Join online communities strategically. BiggerPockets, local Facebook groups, and market-specific forums are valuable if used correctly. Don't lurk. Contribute. Answer questions where you have knowledge. Share your experiences, both successes and failures. Ask thoughtful questions when you need input.

Over time, you'll build reputation in these communities. Other investors will recognize your name. Private messages will start appearing with opportunities, partnership ideas, and off-market deals. This doesn't happen overnight, but it happens if you're consistent and valuable.

Build relationships with multiple contractors before you need them. Don't wait until you have a property to start looking for contractors. Attend local meetups and ask other investors for referrals. Call contractors and introduce yourself. Explain that you're building a portfolio and want to establish relationships before you have urgent needs.

Most good contractors appreciate this approach. They'd rather work with organized clients who plan ahead than desperate clients calling at the last minute. Having three contractors in each category (plumbing, electrical, HVAC, general contracting) means you always have backup options when your primary guy is unavailable or when you need competitive bids.

Connect with lenders proactively. Don't wait until you've found a property to start talking to lenders. Reach out to three to five lenders who specialize in investment property. Ask about their loan programs, rates, requirements, and timelines. Get pre-approved even if you're not ready to buy yet.

This accomplishes several things: you understand your buying power, you know what documents you'll need when it's time to close, and you've started a relationship with people who can close deals quickly when opportunities appear. Fast financing often wins deals in competitive markets.

The pattern here is consistent: build relationships before you need them, contribute value without expecting immediate returns, and stay connected over time. The investors who do this end up with networks that bring them opportunities, solve problems, and create advantages that isolated investors don't have.

Building a Team That Supports Growth

You can't scale alone. At some point, you'll need to build a team. Here's who you need:

Real estate agent: Someone who specializes in investment properties and knows your market. (*investor friendly/investor focused*)

Lender: A loan officer who understands investor loans and can get you pre-approved quickly.

CPA: An accountant who specializes in real estate and can help you maximize deductions and plan for taxes.

Real estate attorney: Someone who can review contracts, handle entity formation, and represent you if there are legal issues.

Property manager: Once you own enough properties or live far from them, a good property manager becomes essential.

Contractors: A reliable handyman, plumber, electrician, and HVAC technician. Having go-to people saves time and stress.

Insurance agent: Someone who understands investment property insurance and can help you get proper coverage.

You don't need all of these on day one. Start with an agent and a lender. Add others as you scale and your needs become more complex.

And remember: your team works for you. Don't be intimidated.

Ask questions. Get multiple opinions. Make sure you understand their advice before following it.**How to Evaluate and Work With Service Providers**

Not all agents, lenders, inspectors, contractors, and property managers are created equal. Learning to evaluate these professionals quickly and objectively saves time and prevents expensive mistakes.

For agents, ask these questions:

How many investment properties have you worked with in the past year? You want someone with regular investor clients, not someone who mostly works with owner-occupants. Investor deals move faster, have different priorities, and require different expertise.

What's your average time from listing to close for investment properties? Fast agents can market and close deals in 30 to 45 days. Slow agents take 60 to 90 days or more. If you're selling, time matters.

Can you provide contact information for three recent investor clients? Talk to these clients. Ask about communication, deal flow, market knowledge, and whether they'd work with the agent again.

For lenders, ask:

What's your average time from application to closing for investment properties? Good lenders close in 30 days or less. Slow lenders take 45 to 60 days, which can cost you deals in competitive markets.

What percentage of your loans are investment properties? You want a lender who specializes in investor loans, not someone who does one or two per year and treats them like owner-occupied mortgages.

What happens if the appraisal comes in low or if issues arise during underwriting? Experienced lenders have contingency plans and can problem-solve quickly. Inexperienced lenders panic or delay, putting your deal at risk.

For inspectors, ask:

How long have you been inspecting properties, and how many do you inspect per year? You want someone with at least five years of experience and at least 200 inspections per year. This ensures they've seen enough properties to spot issues less experienced inspectors miss.

Can you provide a sample inspection report? Review the report for thoroughness. Good inspectors produce detailed reports with photos, descriptions, and recommendations. Poor inspectors produce thin reports that miss critical issues.

Do you specialize in any particular property types? If you're buying old properties, find an inspector with experience in older homes. If you're buying multifamily, find someone familiar with commercial systems.

For contractors, ask:

How long have you been in business, and can you provide proof of licensing and insurance? Never work with unlicensed or uninsured contractors. If they get injured on your property or cause damage, you're liable.

Can you provide references from three recent projects similar to mine? Call these references. Ask about quality, timeliness, communication, and whether the contractor stayed within budget.

What's your typical timeline for a project like mine, and what factors could cause delays? Realistic contractors will give you a range and explain what variables might affect the schedule. Unrealistic contractors will promise fast turnarounds they can't deliver.

For property managers, ask:

How many properties do you manage, and what types? You want someone managing at least 50 properties, preferably properties similar to yours. Too few properties means they're inexperienced or struggling. Too many means they might be stretched thin.

What's your average vacancy time, and how do you market properties? Good property managers should fill vacancies in 15 to 21 days on average. Ask to see examples of their listings. Are they professional? Do they showcase properties well?

How do you handle maintenance and emergencies? They should have established contractor relationships, clear response time commitments, and a system for getting owner approval on major expenses. If they're vague about these processes, they don't have good systems.

The common thread in all these evaluations is specificity. Ask specific questions that require detailed answers. Vague answers indicate inexperience or lack of systems. Detailed, confident answers indicate competence and reliability.

Negotiating With Agents

Many new investors are intimidated by agents. They assume the agent has all the power and knowledge. That's not true, especially when you're a serious buyer.

Here's how to work with agents effectively:

Be clear about your criteria from the start: Share your buy box. Tell them exactly what you're looking for. The clearer you are, the less time they waste showing you properties that don't fit.

Prove you're serious: Get pre-approved before you start looking. Show agents you have financing and reserves. Agents prioritize buyers who can actually close.

Move fast: When a property fits your criteria, act quickly. Schedule showings same day if possible. Make offers within 24 to 48 hours. Agents love working with decisive buyers.

Communicate directly: Don't play games. If you're not interested, say so. If you have concerns, voice them. Agents appreciate straight talk.

Close deals: The fastest way to build credibility is to actually buy properties. Once you've closed a few deals with an agent, they'll prioritize you because they know you follow through.

Provide feedback: When you pass on a property, tell the agent why. This helps them understand your criteria better and bring you more suitable properties.

Over time, you'll build a reputation. Agents will know you're serious, and they'll call you first when they have properties that fit your profile.

When to Fire Service Providers and How to Do It

Even with careful vetting, sometimes service providers don't work out. Knowing when to fire them and how to do it professionally is important.

Fire agents when: they consistently bring you properties outside your buy box after you've communicated your criteria clearly, they don't respond to calls or emails within 24 hours, they pressure you to offer on properties that don't meet your criteria, or they're unavailable when you need to move fast on an opportunity.

How to fire them: "I appreciate your help, but I've decided to work with an agent who specializes more in the property types and neighborhoods I'm targeting. Thank you for your time." Keep it professional. Don't burn bridges. The real estate world is small.

Fire contractors when: they consistently miss deadlines without communication, their work quality is poor, they fail to pull permits when required, they're stealing things, they are showing signs of impairment during work hours, or they aren't responsive to calls and emails when problems arise.

How to fire them: "I'm not satisfied with how this project is going. I'm going to bring in another contractor to finish the work. Here's payment for the work completed to date." Document everything. Take photos. Get written agreements on what's been paid and what work remains. If there's a significant dispute, consult an attorney.

Fire property managers when: vacancy time exceeds 30 days regularly, they're not sending monthly financial reports, they're approving major expenses without your permission, tenant quality is declining, or properties aren't being maintained to your standards.

How to fire them: Review your management agreement for termination clauses. Typically, either party can terminate with 30 to 60 days' written notice. Send formal written notice via email and certified mail. Arrange for transfer of security deposits, keys, tenant files, and financial records. "I've decided to take management in-house" or "I'm transitioning to another management company" is sufficient explanation.

The key to professional terminations is documentation and communication. Don't ghost service providers or suddenly stop working with them without explanation. Be direct, professional, and clear. Most will appreciate the honesty and the relationship won't end badly.

The Long-Term Value of Industry Relationships

The biggest benefit of working well with industry professionals isn't the first deal or the second deal. It's the compounding effect over years.

When you've bought three or four properties with the same agent, they know exactly what you want. They call you before properties hit the MLS. They negotiate harder for you because they know you'll close. They connect you with other investors, lenders, and contractors in their network.

When you've worked with the same lender on multiple deals, they process your applications faster. They advocate for you in underwriting. They give you better rates because you're a repeat customer they trust.

When you've used the same contractors repeatedly, they prioritize your jobs. They give you better prices. They're available for emergencies because they know you're a good client who pays promptly and doesn't create drama.

When you've worked with the same property manager for years, they understand your properties intimately. They know your standards. They handle issues without bothering you because they know what decisions you'll make.

These relationships become assets. They create competitive advantages. They make the business easier and more profitable over time.

The investors who churn through service providers constantly, always looking for someone slightly cheaper or slightly better, never build these advantages. They're always starting from scratch, always explaining their needs, always uncertain about quality.

The investors who find good service providers and stick with them build momentum. Deals come easier. Operations run smoother. Problems get solved faster. This is the real value of working with the industry rather than against it.

13

Chapter 13: Becoming Part of the Industry

At some point, you might consider getting your real estate license. Not because you want to become an agent, but because it gives you tools, access, and optionality that non-licensed investors don't have.

This isn't for everyone. But for some investors, especially those who plan to scale aggressively, it's a smart move.

Why Some Investors Should Get Licensed

There are a few reasons to get licensed:

<u>Access to the MLS:</u> You can search properties yourself without relying on an agent. You see listings the moment they go live.

<u>Save on commissions:</u> If you represent yourself, you earn the

buyer's side commission, usually 2.5 to 3%. On a $300,000 property, that's $7,500 to $9,000 back in your pocket.

<u>Represent other people:</u> If someone wants to sell and you can't buy, you can represent them and earn a commission. You're not just an investor anymore. You're a licensed agent who can facilitate deals even when you're not the buyer.

<u>Networking and credibility:</u> Being licensed gives you access to agent-only events, MLS access, and a level of credibility that opens doors.

Volume Creates Opportunities

Once you're licensed, every conversation becomes a potential transaction. Someone mentions they're thinking about selling? You can represent them. Another investor is looking for deals? You can help them and earn a commission if they buy.

Volume creates opportunities. The more people you talk to, the more deals you'll see. Some of those deals you'll buy. Some you'll broker. Some you'll pass on. But you're in the flow, and that's valuable.

Not Every Contact Becomes a Deal, But You Still Get Paid

Here's the beauty of being licensed: you don't have to buy every property you see. If someone has a property that doesn't fit your buy box but it's a good deal for someone else, you can broker it.

You still get paid. You didn't tie up capital, but you earned a commission. And you helped someone else solve a problem.

This is vertical integration. You're not just an investor. You're also a facilitator. You have more ways to make money from the same deal flow.

It's Not for Everyone

Getting licensed requires time and money. You have to take classes, pass a test, and maintain your license. You have to follow regulations and disclose your license status when you transact.

If you're only planning to buy a few properties over the next decade, licensing probably isn't worth it. But if you're planning to buy 20, 30, 50 properties, or if you want to build a business around real estate, licensing can be a force multiplier.

Building a Team That Supports Growth

You can't scale alone. At some point, you'll need to build a team. Here's who you need:

Real estate agent: Someone who specializes in investment properties and knows your market. (*investor friendly/investor* _focused_)

Lender: A loan officer who understands investor loans and can get you pre-approved quickly.

CPA: An accountant who specializes in real estate and can help you maximize deductions and plan for taxes.

Real estate attorney: Someone who can review contracts, handle entity formation, and represent you if there are legal issues.

Property manager: Once you own enough properties or live far from them, a good property manager becomes essential.

Contractors: A reliable handyman, plumber, electrician, and HVAC technician. Having go-to people saves time and stress.

Insurance agent: Someone who understands investment property insurance and can help you get proper coverage.

You don't need all of these on day one. Start with an agent and a lender. Add others as you scale and your needs become more complex.

And remember: your team works for you. Don't be intimidated. Ask questions. Get multiple opinions. Make sure you understand their advice before following it.

14

Chapter 14: Conclusion

The goal isn't to beat the industry. It's to understand it well enough to use it.

> *Real estate is not a zero-sum game. You don't win by cutting everyone else out. You win by understanding how the system works and using it to your advantage.*

Agents, lenders, contractors, property managers: these people are resources like tools. Good ones make your life easier, save you money, and help you scale. Bad ones cost you time and money. Your job is to find the good ones and build relationships that last.

The real estate industry has inefficiencies. It has bad actors. It has outdated practices. But it also has structure, liquidity, and scale that you can't replicate on your own.

The smartest investors don't fight the industry. They learn how to work with it, when to work around it, and when to become part of it.

That's how you build a portfolio that lasts.

Real estate rewards people who move deliberately, think clearly, and stay disciplined. Everything you need to know is in this book. Now go build something.

Staying Educated and Adapting

Real estate changes. Markets shift. Laws evolve. Strategies that worked five years ago might not work today. The investors who thrive are the ones who keep learning.

Here's how to stay current:

Read consistently: Books, blogs, podcasts. Dedicate 30 minutes a day to real estate education. Focus on practical content, not motivational fluff.

Track your numbers: Review your portfolio monthly. What's working? What's not? Where are you making money? Where are you losing it? Let data guide your decisions.

Attend conferences: Once a year, invest in a real estate conference. The networking alone is worth it. You'll meet investors from other markets and learn strategies you can adapt.

Join mastermind groups: Small groups of investors who meet

regularly to share challenges and solutions. These provide accountability and collective wisdom.

Experiment cautiously: Try new strategies on a small scale before going all-in. Want to try BRRRR? Do it with one property first. Want to invest in a new market? Start with one property and see how it goes.

Learn from mistakes: When something goes wrong, figure out why. Don't just move on. Analyze what happened and how to avoid it next time.

The investors who plateau are the ones who stop learning. They figure out one strategy, repeat it for years, and wonder why their results decline. Markets change. You have to change with them.

Your Path Forward

You've now read a comprehensive guide to real estate investing. You understand how investors think, how to find and analyze deals, how to finance purchases, how to manage properties, how to scale, and how to work with the industry.

But knowledge without action is worthless.

Here's what to do next:

Define your goals. Write them down. Be specific. What do you want real estate to do for you?

Build your buy box. Make it detailed. Share it with agents and your network.

Analyze properties. Get comfortable with the numbers. Learn what good deals look like in your market.

Build your team. Find an agent and a lender. Start those relationships.

Make offers. You'll probably lose the first few. That's fine. Keep going.

Buy your first property. It won't be perfect. That's okay. You'll learn more from owning one property than from analyzing a hundred.

Manage it well. Build systems. Track your numbers. Treat it like a business.

Evaluate after one year. What worked? What didn't? What would you do differently?

Then decide: do you want to scale, stay steady, or exit? Adjust your strategy accordingly.

Real estate is not a get-rich-quick scheme. It's a proven path to wealth for people who are willing to learn, stay disciplined, and think long-term.

You have everything you need to start. Now it's up to you.

Go build something.

APPENDIX: Decision Tree for New Investors

Before you buy your first property, answer these questions. Your answers will shape your strategy.

What kind of investor are you building toward?

I want replacement income in 10 to 15 years

Focus on cash flow and debt paydown. Buy properties in stable markets where rents cover all expenses and provide a cushion. Prioritize paying down mortgages over scaling aggressively. In 15 years, you'll own properties free and clear that generate significant monthly income.

Strategy: Buy 1 to 2 properties per year in affordable markets. Use 30-year mortgages but make extra principal payments when possible. Focus on stability over growth.

Property types: Single-family homes, duplexes, small multi-family in secondary or tertiary markets.

Target returns: 6 to 8% cash-on-cash, stable rents, low vacancy.

I want to grow equity fast and scale

Focus on forced appreciation and refinancing. Buy properties that need work, add value through rehab, refinance to pull your money out, and repeat. This is higher risk and requires more active management, but it scales faster.

Strategy: BRRRR method. Buy below market, improve, refinance, repeat. Target 2 to 3 properties per year once the system is working.

Property types: Single-family homes, small multifamily that need cosmetic or moderate rehab.

Target returns: 8 to 12% cash-on-cash post-refinance, 20 to 30% equity creation through forced appreciation.

I want optionality and low stress

Focus on stable markets and conservative leverage. Buy properties that cash flow well, keep leverage under 70%, and build reserves aggressively. You're not trying to maximize returns. You're trying to build a resilient portfolio that doesn't keep you up at night.

Strategy: Buy 1 property per year. Maintain high equity positions, 30% or more. Build 12 months of reserves per property.

Property types: Turnkey single-family or small multifamily in stable, low-volatility markets.

Target returns: 5 to 7% cash-on-cash, stability over growth.

I'm not sure yet

Start with one property. See what you learn. See whether you like managing tenants, dealing with repairs, and analyzing deals. Your second property should be informed by what you learned from the first.

Strategy: Buy one property that fits conservative criteria. Manage it yourself for at least one year. Then decide if you want to scale, hold steady, or exit.

Final Checklist Before You Buy

Before you make an offer on your first property, make sure you can answer yes to these questions:

1. Have I built a clear buy box?

2. Does this property fit my buy box?

3. Have I analyzed the deal conservatively, low rent estimates, high expense estimates, realistic vacancy?

4. Does it cash flow at least $200 per month after all expenses?

5. Do I have 6 or more months of reserves for this property?

6. Do I have financing lined up and approved?

7. Have I inspected the property or had it professionally inspected?

8. Do I understand the tenant situation, if occupied?

9. Have I researched the neighborhood and market?

10. Can I afford to hold this property if it sits vacant for 3 months?

If you answered no to any of these, pause. Go back and address the gap before you move forward.

This is your guide. Use it. Revise it as you learn. And most importantly: **take action.**

Real estate rewards people who move deliberately, think clearly, and stay disciplined. Everything you need to know is in this book. Now go build your portfolio.